A Manual of
Organizational Know-How

LEADERSHIP
LOGIC

THE FEDERATION OF JEWISH
WOMEN'S ORGANIZATIONS OF MARYLAND
1916-2006

Web Address: www.jewishwomensfed.org

Copyright © 1974, 2000, 2006

ACKNOWLEDGMENTS

The Federation of Jewish Women's Organizations of Maryland wishes to thank:

❖ OTTENHEIMER PUBLISHERS, INC. for assistance and advice in making this publication possible.

❖ Lois B. Rosenfield, Helene H. Waranch and Eleanor J. Hirsh, volunteer and professsional community leaders, for serving as consultants to the committee.

❖ The many individuals and organizations who have served as mentors and role models from whom we have learned and with whom we have shared leadership and friendship throughout the years.

❖ The editorial committees of the 1974 and 2000 editions of LEADERSHIP LOGIC on which this edition is based, revised and enlarged.

Editorial Committee (1974)
Lillian W. Forman
Bernice S. Friedmann
Marion M. Halperin
Marie G. Hammerman
Sara F. Kappelman Harris
Mona M. Wood
Shoshanah S. Cardin and E.B. Hirsh, Co-chairmen

Editorial Committee (2000)
Carol J. Caplan
Janice C. Gold
Hilda W. Hillman
Annafaye W. Joffe
Arlene F. Mazer
E.B. Hirsh, Chairman

FOREWORD

LEADERSHIP LOGIC is intended as a guide toward more effective leadership and more involved membership in all phases and fields of organizational activity. In today's society, with increasing citizen participation and group action, it is vital that all who aspire to leadership, or who find themselves in positions of leadership, achieve a degree of efficiency and expertise.

LEADERSHIP LOGIC is designed for use by leaders of many different kinds of groups: volunteer and professional associations; non-profits such as health agencies, schools, cultural and religious institutions; corporate, condominium and cooperative housing boards; fraternal, social and civic organizations.

LEADERSHIP LOGIC's clear, direct format combines theory with practical application, making it useful for beginning leaders and a handy reference for more experienced leaders to enhance their leadership skills. The information included can be modified to make it compatible with an individual organization's size and needs. In addition, many sections can be adapted for workshops or seminars focused on various facets of leadership training.

Editorial Committee
2006 Edition, revised and expanded, by E.B. Hirsh
Prepared for publication by Jane Isaacs Davis
Carol J. Caplan   Arlene F. Mazer
Janice C. Gold   Helene H. Waranch

Mission Statement
The Federation of Jewish Women's Organizations of Maryland is an umbrella group of non-profit organizations and sisterhoods, committed to leadership training, support of the Jewish community and advocacy of issues of major concern.

LEADERSHIP LOGIC is dedicated to the thousands of volunteer and professional individuals who give of themselves freely and continually – their time and talents, their knowledge and financial support – to improve the quality of life for us all and our communities.

TABLE OF CONTENTS

* "Chairman" and "Chairmen" are used as generic titles throughout this volume, not as gender descriptive.

LEADERSHIP

Leadership is the process of influencing people to cooperate toward attaining goals which they have come to find desirable. *
Effective leadership consists of a number of skills and techniques which can be learned and can be improved by experience.
The leadership team includes officers, board members and those who chair and/or co-chair committees together with executive staff where applicable.

Functions: to educate, motivate, coordinate, establish and work toward accomplishing goals.

1.   On group level
   - To bring goals and performance closer together.
   - To make decisions, establish policies and procedures, implement action, evaluate results.
2.   On individual level
   - To invite, motivate and encourage membership involvement.
   - To channel abilities, interests, energies and expertise of members toward personal fulfillment and organizational achievement.

Responsibilities

1. Know and understand the organization: its background and history, bylaws and policies.
2. Support and promote its mission and objectives, personally and financially.
3. Build and maintain a positive image of the group, both within its membership and the community.
4. Represent the organization, interpret its goals.
5. Identify, encourage, utilize the talents, expertise and experience of members.
6. Establish priorities, evaluate activities, and be receptive to change.
7. Include membership in decision-making, implementation, future planning.
8. Learn the basics of meeting management, parliamentary procedure, public relations and speaking in public.

---

* from Ordway Tead

9. Develop future leadership:
   - Promote and publicize purposes and activities of the organization.
   - Create interest and enthusiasm of members in a climate of acceptance and encouragement.
   - Provide opportunities for involvement and personal growth of others in sharing responsibilities.
   - Plan programs and projects to meet the needs of members: socially, intellectually, emotionally and spiritually.

Duties

1. Plan, prepare for and conduct meetings for which you are responsible; have a written agenda, arrange for record keeping (see SAMPLE AGENDA, Appendix II).
2. Keep notebooks of office up-to-date for continuity and reference.
3. Be prepared to present written and/or oral reports of activities.
4. Transfer promptly and in good order all records, correspondence and relevant materials to successor.

Attitudes

1. Commitment to the organization, its values and goals.
2. Realistic acceptance of leadership role in performing and delegating duties and responsibilities.
3. Genuine concern and respect for people: acceptance, sensitivity and empathy.
4. Willingness to share the limelight: to give credit for ideas, knowledge, skills and achievements of others.
5. Receptivity to new ideas, suggestions and criticism.
6. Understanding the need for continuity: knowledge of the past, commitment to the present, concern for the future.

Techniques for developing future leadership

1. For officers:
   - Involvement in executive sessions: planning, decision-making, goal-setting and evaluation meetings.
   - Participation in various aspects of the organization's activities.
   - Attendance at leadership skills workshops.
   - Opportunities to demonstrate leadership abilities.

---

* "Chairman" and "Chairmen" are used as generic titles throughout this volume, not as gender descriptive.

2. For board members and committee chairmen:*
   - Orientation sessions and skills workshops.
   - Involvement in decision-making, goal-setting and evaluation on a committee level.
   - Opportunities to chair working committees of at least three people, to share and delegate responsibility.
   - Recognition of work accomplished: praise publicly, "suggest" privately.
   - Service in various capacities; development and maintenance of committee files.
   - Opportunities for personal growth: the study and use of materials provided by national, regional and local groups.
3. For members on all levels, provide:
   - Meaningful, challenging, do-able tasks.
   - Encouragement and support.
   - Tools and techniques for success.
   - Recognition for performance and achievement.

Rewards and Benefits of Leadership
1. Personal achievement and satisfaction through using talents, abilities, expertise.
2. Increased self-confidence and enhancement of skills in organizational management.
3. Identification as a representative of the organization: its goals, activities, membership and accomplishments.
4. Public recognition as an aware, concerned, involved individual.
5. Development of community perspective: increased awareness of community programs, personnel and needs.
6. Formation of personal friendships and working relationships with diverse individuals and groups.
7. Acquisition of new skills, techniques and insights.
8. Greater understanding and commitment to the organization, its mission and effectiveness.

Pitfalls of Leadership
1. Over-personalizing the organizational role; reacting on the "I" level.
2. Unrealistic expectation of self and others; inability to see things as they are.
3. Abuse of power, misinterpretation of authority.
4. Fears: of being judged, of losing popularity, of failure.

5. Tendency to rationalize, seek excuses, blame others, claim ignorance.
6. Inability to delegate effectively; tendency to "micromanage."

MEMBERSHIP

People join organizations for many reasons, primarily because of their interest in supporting and being identified with the mission, goals and members of groups that meet their needs. Membership committees are charged with recruiting, involving and retaining members.

Rights
1. Know mission, goals, bylaws and policies of the organization.
2. Attend meetings, participate in activities.
3. Receive reports of programs, projects and progress of group's activities.
4. Help choose leadership: nominate and elect.
5. Aspire to leadership; become a candidate for election.

Responsibilities
1. Meet membership requirements as stated in the bylaws; pay dues promptly.
2. Promote goals and purposes of the organization.
3. Support activities and projects with time, effort and funds.
4. Attend meetings regularly, and on time.
5. Read communications received; respond as required.
6. Take part in debate; voice ideas and opinions.
7. Learn basic parliamentary procedure.
8. Serve on committees; share knowledge, talents, expertise.
9. Respect rights of all; abide by will of the majority.
10. Accept leadership role when asked.
11. If resignation becomes necessary, do so in writing to facilitate action.

Rewards and benefits

1. Personal growth and fulfillment; opportunities for involvement, service, recognition.
2. Opportunities to develop and enhance leadership skills.
3. Shared interests, talents, skills, expertise.
4. Identification with group and its accomplishments.
5. Broadened horizons, experiences and knowledge.
6. Development of personal relationships, friendships.
7. Feeling accepted, needed, valued.
8. Awareness of community needs and issues; involvement in programs and projects that benefit individuals and the community.

Strategies for membership recruitment, renewal, retention, integration and involvement

1. Personal contact is the key to membership growth, maintenance and involvement.
2. The best marketing tool is the scope and variety of programs of all kinds: decision-making meetings; social, educational, cultural, fundraising events; advocacy, service projects, etc.
3. A membership committee made up of members representative of diverse age and interest groups.
   - Prepare job description for each facet of the work.
   - Target specific prospective, potential members.
   - Issue phone or handwritten invitations to join, attend together, learn about the group; why "we need you!"
   - Tea, luncheon, reception to meet leadership and staff; showcase the organization.
   - Mailings, newsletters that describe activities and accomplishments, sell the organization, invite membership.
   - State benefits of joining: personally, organizationally and community wide.
4. Incentives for joining.
   - Free first year membership.
   - Paid-up membership event.
   - Personal sponsorship, mentoring of new members.
   - Special interest, affinity groups.
5. New member events, activities.
   - Use "icebreakers."
   - Meet and greet, welcome, introduce new members.
   - Furnish name tags, calendar of year's events.
   - Showcase organization's accomplishments, meet leadership and staff, tour facilities.

- Promote sense of belonging, being accepted, needed.
- Provide and distribute membership profile survey to ascertain areas of interests, talents, expertise, etc.
- Encourage volunteering, serving on committees; invite participation based on stated interests.
- Recognize, praise, honor volunteer participation.

6. Phonathons for recruiting, renewing and retaining members.
   - Choose and train callers.
   - Prepare and assign prospect cards.
   - Arrange timing and place.
   - Provide caller "response cards."
   - Schedule a report meeting; evaluate results, make recommendations.
9. Continue to involve, motivate long-time members.
10. Recycle seasoned leaders as mentors, advisors.

FORMING AN ORGANIZATION

An organization as used herein is a group of people with common interests and concerns who meet to determine action and/or activities to be taken in the name of the group.

Call to the initial meeting
1. Notify/invite people who are thought to be in agreement with the purpose(s); include time, place, reason for the meting.
2. Seek advice of someone with organizational experience.
3. Prepare, in advance, a statement of purpose.

The initial meeting
1. Call to order by one of the initiators, stating purpose of meeting.
2. Elect a temporary chairman ("chairman pro tem").
3. Elect a temporary secretary ("secretary pro tem").
4. Read notice of meeting for inclusion in the minutes.

5. Draft a statement of purpose, the reason(s) for establishing the group.
   Ex.: "It is the sense of this meeting that (<u>name</u>) shall be formed for the purpose of _____".
6. Discuss, develop, agree on a mission statement and proposed activities of the group.
7. Establish a bylaws committee to draft bylaws and report back.
8. Call for other business.
9. Move to adjourn to (<u>date</u>), (<u>time</u>), (<u>place</u>).
10. Adjourn.

The second meeting
1. Call to order (by chairman pro tem).
2. Present minutes of initial meeting (by secretary pro tem).
3. Report of bylaws committee.
   a. Have copies available for all in attendance, if possible.
   b. Present each paragraph in order, one at a time, for discussion and amendment.
   c. Ask for any further amendments.
4. Vote on bylaws in entirety; majority vote required for acceptance.
5. Recess for attendees to sign sheet attached to bylaws; all who sign are "charter members" and entitled to vote.
6. Call meeting to order (president pro tem).
7. Read names of those entitled to vote.
8. Elect permanent officers according to bylaws just adopted.
   a. Election by open nominating and election procedure,
      OR
   b. Recess for nominating committee to meet and prepare a slate; reconvene to elect,
      OR
   c. Adjourn to another date to receive the nominating committee report and for the election to take place.
9. Newly elected officers replace temporary officers.
10. Call for further business such as appointment of committees and date of next meeting.
11. Adjourn.

DEVELOPING A MISSION STATEMENT

A mission statement is an affirmation or reaffirmation of the organization's purpose(s). It provides the framework (with the bylaws) of the group's overall programming and activities, values and vision.

Procedures
1. Appoint a committee representative of the membership.
2. Examine present mission statement and bylaws.
3. Compare current activities with these documents.
   a. Are they compatible?
   b. Has the membership changed? The values? The issues? The activities?
   c. Are there inconsistencies?
4. Brainstorm to reach group decisions.
   a. Direction setting based on membership profile and concerns.
   b. Values and vision based on realistic expectations.
5. Compose a preliminary statement; study and evaluate it.
6. Prepare a final draft; present the statement for adoption by the board and /or membership.

Principles
1. Should be concise, realistic.
2. Should be general to allow for some flexibility.
3. Should be easily understood and accepted.
4. Should reflect and affect the group's activities and goals.
5. Should be formulated, as a long-range plan, to be a guide for the next 3-5 years.

BYLAWS

Bylaws are the established set of rules and procedures by which an organization is governed.

Purposes

1. To state fundamental principles for administration of the group.
2. To establish the basic structure and rules of operation of an organization, its framework for action.

Adopting and amending bylaws

1. Adoption of original bylaws requires a majority vote of those eligible to vote who are present and voting.
2. Amendments allow for changing the framework to meet challenges and changes of time and focus.
   a. Amending previously adopted bylaws is a formal procedure requiring a two-thirds vote of the membership, prior notice having been given.
   b. Interpreting, implementing bylaws can be accomplished less formally by establishing policies or standing rules to further define bylaws requirements.
   c. Amending such policies requires a majority vote of those present and voting at a board or membership meeting without prior notice.

Suggested outline of basic bylaws (see SAMPLE BYLAWS, Appendix I)

ARTICLE I.	Name.
ARTICLE II.	Object, goals, purposes.
ARTICLE III.	Membership: eligibility, classes of membership, dues.
ARTICLE IV.	Officers: list of officers, eligibility for office, nomination and election, term(s) of office, duties, vacancies in office.
ARTICLE V.	Board of Directors: personnel, election procedure, terms of office, duties, meetings, quorum, filling vacancies.
ARTICLE VI.	Executive Committee: personnel, duties, meetings, quorum.

POLICY, STANDING RULES

Written policy (standing rules) includes procedures enacted to implement bylaws requirements as well as procedures established through custom and tradition.

Purposes
1.   To interpret, further define bylaws requirements.
2.   To provide for efficiency and continuity of operation.
3.   To allow greater flexibility for change than amending the bylaws.
4.   To reflect current practice and provide for future needs.

Procedures
1.   To be established and/or revised as needed, then appended to the bylaws.
2.   May be adopted by majority vote at a general or board meeting without prior notice.
3.   May be amended by 2/3 vote at a general or board meeting without prior notice.

NOMINATIONS AND ELECTIONS

Nominations are proposals naming persons as candidates for specific positions in an organization; election to office is by vote of members entitled to vote. Methods of nominating are usually prescribed in bylaws (often by a nominating committee); otherwise, the method is chosen by vote (from the floor, by committee or by ballot).

A Nominating Committee

1. Purposes
   a. To prepare a slate of candidates for office to be presented for election at a specified meeting.
   b. To fill vacancies among officers and board members as they occur, in accordance with bylaws.
   c. A standing nominating committee functioning year round provides opportunities for its members to seek and observe potential leaders: to recognize talents, expertise, commitment, leadership abilities.
2. Members
   a. Appointed and/or elected according to bylaws.
   b. Representative of cross-section of membership.
   c. Immediate past chairman as ex-officio member is recommended.
   d. Members of the committee may be nominated unless stated otherwise in bylaws or policy.
3. Duties
   a. Understand the organization and its needs, the members and their talents, interests and needs.
   b. Know the offices and vacancies to be filled, qualifications desired, duties to be performed, including job descriptions.
   c. Outline responsibilities realistically to prospective candidates; do not undersell the responsibilities, or pressure a reluctant nominee.
      - Must be able to attend meetings.
      - Must be available to accept an area of responsibility.
   d. Place a name in nomination only with prior consent of the individual.
   e. Present report to the board and/or membership in accordance with bylaws.

Election Procedures

1. The presiding officer: president presides unless president's name appears on the slate, in which case the chair should be relinquished to the first vice-president; if both names are on the slate, another vice-president or the secretary may preside.

2. The nominating committee report is presented by the chairman.

3. If bylaws do not provide for nominations from the floor,

    a. The nominating committee chairman may state: "Since no additional nominations have been received and the bylaws do not allow for nominations from the floor, I move (on behalf of the nominating committee) that the slate of nominees be elected to office." The presiding officer: "If there is no objection, the slate will be voted on in its entirety." (If there is any objection, each candidate must be voted on separately). The vote is taken and announced.

    OR

    b. The presiding officer may state that, since no additional nominations have been received, and if there is no objection (any objection, see above), the vote will be to elect the nominees to office, then call for the vote or instruct the secretary to cast the ballot to elect those individuals to office.

4. If additional nominations are received in writing by the committee or secretary (whichever is designated in the bylaws), the slate is reported as published or announced and the additional nominations read.

    a. If no ballot has been provided, the presiding officer calls for vote by voice or by show of hands, naming the nominees for each office in order.

    b. The candidate(s) with the largest number of votes is elected.

5. Nominations from the floor

    a. If bylaws provide for nominations from the floor, the presiding officer reads slate, an office at a time, asking if there are further nominations.

    b. If there are further nominations, vote is called for on candidates for each office beginning with the office of president; candidate for each office with the largest number of votes is elected.

6.   Election by ballot
   a.   May be prescribed in bylaws or decided by majority vote.
   b.   Form: prepared ballots list the names of candidates with spaces for voters' choices, or blank slips of paper may be distributed for choices to be indicated.
   c.   Procedure
      - Tellers appointed to distribute, collect, count the ballots and report the vote.
      - Ballots deposited in receptacle(s) passed by tellers or in a ballot box.
      - Tellers retire to count the votes; then report number of votes for each candidate.
      - Presiding officer receives the report, announces the results.

7.   Newly elected officers may take office immediately or after being installed, according to bylaws or custom. (See Installations, page 76).

DUTIES OF OFFICERS

The officers of an organization should be designated in the bylaws. The minimum essential officers are a presiding officer and a secretary. However, most organizations operate with a president, vice president(s), recording secretary, corresponding secretary and treasurer.

Officers as role models

1. Believe in, support group's mission, values and vision, programs and projects.
2. Demonstrate commitment in time, funds and effort.
3. Create, encourage atmosphere of mutual trust, confidence, respect.
4. Share knowledge, experience, skills and materials; develop future leaders.
5. Foster good working relationships among members, lay leadership and professional staff, if applicable.

The President as administrative officer

1. Become thoroughly familiar with the mission, bylaws, policies and procedures of the organization; arrange periodic reviews for revisions and amendments as needed.
2. Work closely with professional executive, if applicable.
3. Appoint committee chairmen in accordance with bylaws and policy; consult with chairmen and/or professional in selecting committee members.
4. Work toward increased membership involvement and participation.
5. Arrange for orientation of officers, board members and committee chairmen.
   a. Include overview of the organization:
      - Bylaws, policies, history.
      - Mission, goals, purposes.
      - Activities, programs, projects.
      - Relationship to parent organization and/or other affiliations, if applicable.
   b. Explain organizational procedures:
      - Job descriptions, files and records.
      - Financial framework.
      - Expectations of leaders.

6. Plan for coordination of committee activities.
7. Serve as member, ex-officio, if bylaws so provide, of all committees <u>except</u> the nominating committee; attend major <u>planning</u> meetings, not all <u>working</u> meetings.
8. Review minutes with recording secretary in preparation for presentation; arrange to have minutes approved by committee if reading has been dispensed with at a meeting.
9. Consult with corresponding secretary on all correspondence.
10. Direct mail to proper persons; organizational mail belongs to the group, <u>not</u> to the individual.
11. Schedule meetings; clear dates with community calendars.
12. Sign checks and vouchers as specified in bylaws; do not sign blank checks.
13. Prepare and submit annual report.
14. Transfer promptly and in good order to successor, all records and correspondence; include policies, lists of chairmen and committees, timetable of activities, etc.

The Presiding Officer: *the president, chairman or other designated individual.*
1. Prepare a timed agenda; send copy to vice-president(s), and/or distribute to all board members (see SAMPLE AGENDA, Appendix II,).
2. Notify, in advance, all those who are to give reports.
3. Become familiar with basic Parliamentary Procedure (pages 39-48).
4. Call meeting to order at designated time and, a quorum being present, proceed with business; without a quorum, business that requires no action can proceed: i.e., announcements, program.
5. Announce each item of business in order; remain seated during reports and announcements by others.
6. Refer to self impersonally as "the chair" (or "your president").
7. Recognize members who wish to speak.
   a. Use correct names and titles.
   b. Encourage discussion by individuals, decision by the group.
   c. Keep discussion relevant, objective; avoid personalities.
   d. Observe rules of debate (see page 45).
   e. Keep agenda moving.
8. Supply background information as needed; refrain from expressing personal opinion.
9. State clearly each motion for discussion; after discussion,

repeat the motion, put it to vote; announce result(s).

10. Decide parliamentary questions; seek the advice of the parliamentarian, if one has been designated.

11. Relinquish the chair RARELY:
   a. When desiring to speak to a motion; resume chair after vote has been taken.
   b. When name appears on slate for election.

12. Vote ONLY when voting is by ballot; otherwise, vote to make or break a tie.

13. Adjourn the meeting: the presiding officer may state, "If there is no further business, (pause), and there is no objection, (pause), the meeting is adjourned."

   OR

   A member may move to adjourn, the motion needing a second and a vote.

14. Begin follow-up activities after each meeting.
   a. Thank those responsible for meeting just completed.
   b. Check minutes, correspondence with secretary.
   c. Attend to financial responsibilities.
   d. Coordinate on-going activities.
   e. Plan for the next meeting.

Co-presidents (or presidium): *an arrangement for a shared presidency.*

1. Reasons:
   - Changing lifestyles, population mobility.
   - Reluctance, inability to commit time necessary to accept full responsibility; willingness to share.
   - Need to revitalize an organization, to use/develop experienced leadership; past presidents could be "recycled" or serve as "mentors."

2. Dividing responsibilities
   - By time periods: each serving as the president for part(s) of the term.
   - By job assignment: based on interests, expertise.
   - By sharing all activities: representing the organization, presiding at meetings, sending and receiving communications, sharing funds available for expenses, etc.
   - Workability depends on the individuals.

3. Practical aspects
   - Written policy may state that the term **president** may be understood to include co-presidents, if applicable.
   - Succession to the following presidency is at the discretion of the nominating committee.

The Vice President(s): *the first vice president or president elect is the understudy for the president.*

1. Be aware of, and become familiar with, the duties and responsibilities of the president, and all phases of the organization.
2. Assist the president whenever called upon.
3. Preside in the absence of the president.
4. Represent the organization upon request of the president.
5. Accept responsibility for coordinating various activities of the organization:
   a. To chair an important committee.
   b. To chair or coordinate a department or group of committees.

The Recording Secretary: *an elected officer responsible for recording the proceedings of meetings, the minutes (see SAMPLE MINUTES, Appendix III).*

1. Take minutes which should include:
   a. Type of meeting: regular, board or special.
   b. Name of organization.
   c. Time and date, including year.
   d. Name and title of presiding officer.
   e. Action taken on minutes of previous meeting: whether read or dispensed with; approved or corrected (include corrections).
   f. Correspondence, announcements and reports; action taken on each item.
   g. Treasurer's report; append to minutes and file for audit.
   h. Summary of reports given or reports attached.
   i. All main motions whether carried or lost; omit discussion, refer to it as "after much discussion," etc.
   j. All other motions if carried.
   k. Name of mover, not seconder, unless extremely important issue.
   l. Concise summary of program, if there is one.
   m. Time of adjournment.
   n. Signature: Jane Doe
                   Recording Secretary
                   (Do not end with "Respectfully submitted")
   o. Denote approval of minutes by date and signature. Note: Minutes are the recorded history and legal recording of the organization and, as such, must be accurate for future reference.

2. Prepare the minutes within 7 days and send a copy to the president.
3. Present minutes at the next meeting of the same body, or prepare for distribution.
4. Maintain all minutes and records of the organization which are not specifically assigned to others.
   a. Keep record of attendance.
   b. Keep record books current and have them available at meetings.
5. Present all records promptly and in good order to successor.

The Corresponding Secretary: *an elected officer charged with attending to written communications to and from the organization (see SAMPLE CORRE- SPONDENCE, Appendix IV).*
1. Notify members of executive and board meetings.
2. Consult with the president; present correspondence received since the last meeting, giving name of <u>sender</u> first, then body or essence of letter.
3. Handle all general correspondence promptly with approval of the president.
4. Use official stationery.
5. Type letters with copy for the file; handwrite social notes (congratulations, condolences, etc.)
6. Use correct titles and forms of address (see pages 61-62).
7. Be concise, but complete and to the point.
8. Sign full name and title for identification:
   Mary F. Brown
   Corresponding Secretary

The Treasurer: *an elected officer, custodian of the organization's funds.*
1. Arrange for proper signing of all checks.
   a. Bylaws or policy should provide for two signatures; at least three individuals should be authorized to sign checks.
   b. Never sign blank checks.
2. Serve on budget committee (see SAMPLE BUDGET, Appendix V).
3. Maintain custody of financial records and assets of organization.
4. Receive, deposit, record, account for all money and assets.
   a. Deposit cash; do <u>not</u> use cash to pay bills.
   b. Deposit checks <u>at once</u> after entering the amount and source.

5. Pay and record all bills and vouchers that have been authorized in accordance with bylaws or procedures of the organization.
6. Keep books up-to-date; have available at meetings for reference.
7. Report at board, general and annual meetings.
8. Submit books and records to authorized auditor at end of fiscal year.
9. Transfer promptly and in good order to successor all securities, monies, records and signature cards of the organization.

The Financial Secretary: *may be elected or appointed as prescribed in the bylaws or otherwise authorized by action of the organization.*
1. Maintain accurate membership files.
2. Send membership bills.
3. Receive dues through mail and/or at meetings.
4. Record dues payments on membership records.
5. Transmit funds to treasurer promptly with a report, keeping a copy on file.
6. Report periodically dues collected, number of paid and unpaid members; number of new members, members lost.
7. Notify retention chairman or other designated individual of members delinquent in dues payments according to policy of organization.
8. Transfer promptly and in good order to successor all organization funds, files and records.

The Auditor: *may be elected, appointed, or hired as prescribed in the bylaws or authorized by action of the organization.*
1. Examine treasurer's records, books, vouchers, cancelled checks, bank statements, check stubs, cash accounts, etc.
2. Prepare complete financial statement at close of fiscal year.
3. Submit report: "Books examined and found correct."
   Mary R. Smith, Auditor
   (date)

FINANCIAL FRAMEWORK

Purposes
1. Record and safeguard assets of the organization.
2. Provide the basis for effective business procedures.
3. Give authorized officers the instruments for handling the funds and assets of the organization.
4. Furnish information for policy decisions.
5. Enable members to understand the finances of the organization, the need for funds, and their disbursement.

Authority
1. Financial transactions.
   a. Charter.
   b. Constitution, bylaws, rules of procedure, policy.
   c. Established precedent.
   d. Action, as recorded in the minutes.
2. Disbursements
   a. Budget (see SAMPLE BUDGET, Appendix III,).
   b. Board and/or membership action, as recorded in the minutes.
   c. Approved bills.
   d. Signed vouchers.
3. Bonding is recommended for the protection of the individual as well as the organization.

Financial Statements
1. Statement of assets and liabilities: all funds and assets of the organization.
2. Statement of operations: income and expenses for a given period.
3. Cash flow statement: receipts and disbursements.
4. Evidence of transactions: deposit slips, canceled checks, bank books and statements; receipt books, paid bills, signed vouchers, invoices, pledge cards, etc.
5. Annual or year-end reports must include all accounts, assets and liabilities of the organization.

Budget

1. Definition: a financial plan for raising and allocating funds to meet the projected needs of the organization for a specific period, usually a year at a time.

2. The committee

    a. Suggested personnel: chairman, president, 1st vice-president and treasurer; the immediate past president and treasurer; chairmen of key committees responsible for raising or spending considerable sums of money; and any additional members deemed necessary or desirable.

    b. Procedures

    -   Review past actual income and expenses, especially from the previous year
    -   Compare year-to-date actual income and expenses to the budgeted amounts.
    -   Project income and expenses for the rest of the year in progress.
    -   Evaluate present operations: policies, procedures, treasurers' records.
    -   Devise a plan for the allocation of funds based on anticipated income, knowledge of past performance, policies and commitments, needs and requests for expenditures in the coming fiscal year.
    -   Determine means of raising needed funds for a balanced budget.
    -   Present the proposed budget to the appropriate group (board or membership) for approval.
    -   After adoption, may be reviewed or revised by group action.

THE BOARD OF DIRECTORS

Most organizations are governed by a Board of Directors; the personnel and duties of the Board should be designated in the bylaws. Board members are the shapers and interpreters of the organization, working for the present and planning for the future.

Personnel usually includes one or a combination of:
1. Elected officers, board members, past presidents.
2. Board members appointed for specific duties.
3. Those who chair standing and special committees.
4. The executive director, if there is one.

Functions, Responsibilities
1. Meet regularly; work as a team with enthusiasm and personal support.
2. Establish clear objectives; develop plans for achieving them.
3. Conduct routine business of the organization.
4. Study, formulate, decide, evaluate, administer policies and activities of the organization.
   - Adopt, periodically review bylaws and policies.
   - Determine the mission and purposes, programs and projects, planning and activities of the organization.
   - Monitor and evaluate the group's operations.
5. Accept responsibility for effective fiscal management.
   - Adopt annual operating budget.
   - Authorize and approve annual audit.
   - Establish, monitor, assume responsibility for all expenditures including staff salaries and facilities management, assets and liabilities.
   - Create and oversee income sources to meet organization's needs and goals.
   - Meet tax, insurance, postal and legal requirements.
   - Assume ultimate responsibility for the legal and moral administration of the organization.
6. Make recommendations to the membership for action.
7. Act for the membership between general meetings.
8. Support decisions, activities adopted by majority vote.

9. Recruit, employ, evaluate professional executive director where applicable.
   - Prepare job description.
   - Establish personnel practices.
10. Personnel responsibilities
    - Arrange for recruitment, orientation and development of future leadership.
    - Prepare job descriptions.
    - Encourage involvement of members in all facets of organization's activities.
    - Work, consult, collaborate with staff members.
11. Public relations
    - Promote positive public image of the organization.
    - Advocate for community and current issues that affect or are compatible with the group's mission.
    - Cooperate with other organizations having similar goals.
    - Become knowledgeable of community needs, concerns and developments..

THE EXECUTIVE COMMITTEE

Those organizations which operate with an Executive Committee should specify its personnel and duties in the bylaws; personnel usually limited to elected officers, immediate past president and executive director, if applicable.

Duties
1. Serve as advisory committee to the president.
2. Make recommendations to the board for action.
3. Act in emergency situations.
4. Meet at the call of the president unless otherwise specified in bylaws.

COMMITTEES

A committee is a group of people elected or appointed to consider, investigate and/or take action on a particular matter.

Purposes
1. Provide workable units in which to consider, investigate, recommend and/or perform necessary activities for the organization.
2. Provide for the development of leadership.
3. Provide for shared responsibility.
4. Provide for wide participation and involvement of membership.

Types
1. Standing committees.
    *   Usually listed in bylaws to perform continuing functions.
    *   Serve for a specific term until successors have been chosen.
2. Special or ad hoc committees.
    *   Appointed as needed to carry out specified tasks.
    *   Terminate immediately upon presentation of final report.

Structure
1. Chairmen*: appointed by president in accordance with bylaws and/or policy.
2. Committee members: appointed by president or by committee chairmen in consultation with president; should include:
    *   Minimum of three members.
    *   At least one member of previous committee to allow for continuity.
    *   A co-chairman or vice-chairman to provide for shared responsibility and future leadership.
3. Meetings as necessary to accomplish designated tasks.

---

* "Chairman" and "Chairmen" are used as generic titles throughout this volume, not as gender descriptive.

COMMITTEE CHAIRMEN*

A committee chairman is the presiding officer of a designated committee, be it a standing or special, ad hoc, committee.

Duties
1. Become thoroughly familiar with the committee's "charge," files and records.
2. Understand, promote, support, interpret the mission, activities and goals of the organization and the committee's relationship to its purposes.
3. Consult the president, vice-president in charge and/or past chairman as to members of the committee.
4. Ask committee members to serve, outlining committee's procedures.
5. Ascertain budget allotments and income expectations.
6. Follow established procedures for financial transactions: submission of bills, vouchers, etc.; sign each with name and name of committee.
7. Observe correct procedures for correspondence.
8. Schedule and conduct committee meetings.
   a. Clear dates with appropriate personnel: president and vice-president.
   b. Notify committee members of time and place.
   c. Prepare agenda.
   d. Arrange for minutes of meetings.
   e. Delegate and divide responsibilities among committee members.
      • Coordinate various facets of the work.
      • Give credit, recognition and praise for work accomplished.
   f. Encourage group participation, decision-making and involvement.
   g. Establish deadlines and schedule to do the work.
   h. Help committee determine best way(s) to accomplish the task.
9. Plan for evaluation sessions(s).

---

*"Chairman" and "Chairmen" are used as generic titles throughout this volume, not as gender descriptive.

10. Prepare interim and annual reports as requested (give written reports to recording secretary, especially if numbers, dates and names are included).
11. Notify president, request time for committee reports, especially if discussion of recommendations is expected.
12. Present committee reports that contain recommendations as follows: "The committee recommends that..." OR "On behalf of the committee I move to...or that...." (This technique eliminates calls for a second to the motion; the committee members have been the seconds.)
13. Meet with successor, transfer promptly and in good order committee records, files and other relevant material.

DEPARTMENTALIZATION

A system whereby related committees are grouped together under a coordinator, usually a vice-president or other designated officer or board member.

Purposes
1. Provide for coordination and overview of activities.
2. Relieve president of supervisory details; permit sharing of responsibility.
3. Increase efficiency of operation and communication within the organization, with national and regional offices and the local community.
4. Develop leadership experience and expertise.
5. Group committees or other activities with similar or related purposes; ex: administrative, membership services, projects, programs, etc.

Functions of a Coordinator
1. Work closely with each committee in the department.
2. Act as liaison with other department chairmen for overall coordination of activities.
3. Report to the president, board and membership from time to time.

NOTEBOOKS OF OFFICE

The development and maintenance of records and files, procedure notebooks, are recommended for all officers and committees.

Purposes
1. Provide a job description/committee "charge."
2. Serve as record of procedures, activities and accomplishments of each office/committee, past and present.

Form
1. Loose-leaf book, 8 1/2" x 11" size.
2. Large envelope inside cover for pamphlets, flyers, clippings, photos, etc.
3. File folders.
4. Computer disks.

Contents
1. General.
   - Bylaws and policies of organization.
   - List of officers, board members, chairmen.
   - Directives for submitting bills, making payments and reports.
2. Specifics for committee chairmen.
   - Job description, responsibilities, tasks of the committee.
   - Budget and financial records of the committee.
   - List of committee members.
   - Committee operation including planning, functions and policies.
   - Minutes of committee meetings.
   - Reports: copy of each report given, including annual report.
   - Evaluations and recommendations.
   - Copies of publicity, mailings, correspondence, etc.
   - Materials and information relevant to committee's activities.

A HISTORY OF THE ORGANIZATION

An organization may provide for the appointment or election of an individual as historian to maintain its permanent and current files and scrapbooks.

Purpose
1. Reference and continuity.
2. Recognition of group and individual accomplishments.
3. Special anniversary celebrations.
4. Publicity and promotion.

Contents should include, in chronological order:
1. Charter, bylaws, policies.
2. Lists of officers, board members, committee information and membership rosters.
3. Minute books.
4. Correspondence files, notebooks of office and annual reports.
5. Awards received and presented.
6. All printed publicity, clippings, brochures, bulletins, announcements, etc.
7. Photographs.

Historian's responsibilities
1. Serve as custodian of permanent files to be kept in secure place.
2. Urge/help each president prepare a file of activities and records of that administration.
3. Prepare or arrange for the publication of an official written history.
4. From time to time present interesting items from the history at meetings of the organization.
5. Develop exhibits of materials from the history for meetings and/or publicity purposes.

PARLIAMENTARY PROCEDURE

Parliamentary Procedure, because of its technical language, is usually thought to be complicated and formal. Basically, it is little more than common sense combined with common courtesy; it is democracy in action.

Principles
1. Rights of members.
   - The right of the majority to prevail.
   - The right of the minority to be heard.
   - The right of the absentees to be protected.
2. Orderly transaction of business; consideration of one thing at a time.
3. Courtesy and justice for all.

Parliamentary terms
- ADJOURN: to end a meeting officially.
- ADOPT: to act favorably on a motion, to accept or approve.
- AGENDA: the order of business at a meeting.
- AMEND: to modify or alter a motion or document.
- ASSEMBLY: a group of people gathered for a common purpose to determine courses of action.
- BALLOT: a secret vote.
- BUSINESS: matters brought before an assembly.
- BYLAWS: document listing the basic rules for governing an organization.
- CHAIR (the): refers to the presiding officer.
- ELECTION: the selection of person(s) by vote.
- EX-OFFICIO: by virtue of office; having all the privileges of membership, not the obligations.
- FLOOR (obtain the): to be recognized in order to speak in an assembly.
- GERMANE: related or pertinent to
- MEETING: an assembly of members gathered to transact business.
- MINUTES: the official written record of proceedings of a meeting.
- MOTION: a proposal that brings a matter before a meeting for consideration and action.
- NOMINATION: formally naming a person as a candidate for

election or appointment.
- QUORUM: the minimum number of members entitled to vote that must be present for the legal transaction of business.
- RATIFY: to approve action already taken.
- RECESS: a short intermission within a meeting.
- RECONSIDER: to consider, for a second time, a previously adopted or defeated question.
- RESCIND: to annul action previously adopted.
- RESOLUTION: a formal motion.
- SERIATIM (AD): consideration of a proposal one section or paragraph at a time, as bylaws; vote is on the whole.
- SESSION: a meeting or series of meetings, as a convention, for the transaction of business.
- VOTE: a positive or negative expression of choice or opinion.

The Parliamentarian: *the parliamentarian is a consultant or advisor to the presiding officer on matters of parliamentary procedure, is usually appointed by the president and gives advice or opinion, not decisions.*

Duties/Responsibilities
1. Become familiar with the organization's bylaws and policies.
2. Be available to confer with the presiding officer before meetings to anticipate problems that may arise.
3. Serve as consultant/advisor to members on questions of parliamentary procedure.
4. Be seated next to, or immediately behind, the presiding officer.
5. Call attention, inconspicuously, of presiding officer to any error or question in the proceedings.
6. If a member, the parliamentarian, may vote only when voting is by ballot.

A professional parliamentarian may be retained as a key consultant in preparation for and during a convention.

MOTIONS

All main motions: *present proposals to an assembly for consideration, or may be made following the presentation of a report or other communication.*

Cannot be made if any other motion is pending.
Require a second.
Can be discussed.
Require a majority vote (exceptions noted below).
Vote can be reconsidered.

Resolutions are main motions, usually formal written proposals which may begin with a preamble to give background information on the proposed action (see SAMPLE RESOLUTIONS, Appendix VII).

All subsidiary motions: *assist and pave the way for changing or disposing of a main motion.*

Have precedence over main motions.
Require a second.
Must be voted on before the main motion; if accepted, become part of the main motion to be voted on.

Subsidiary motions in order of precedence from highest ranking to lowest:
1.   Lay on the table – postpone until a later time.
      Cannot be discussed.   Requires a majority vote.
      Cannot be amended.   Cannot be reconsidered.
      To take from the table – requires a main motion.
2.   Previous question – calls for an immediate vote (stops discussion).
      Cannot be discussed.   Requires 2/3 vote.
      Cannot be amended.   Cannot be reconsidered.
      When adopted, the pending question is put to vote immediately.
3.   Limit and/or extend debate or discussion – sets time allowed for discussion.
      Cannot be discussed.   Requires 2/3 vote.
      Can be amended.   Can be reconsidered.

4.   Postpone to a certain time – to consider motion at a definite time in the future.
     Can be discussed.   Requires a majority vote.
     Can be amended.   Can be reconsidered.
5.   Refer to a committee – to have the question considered by a small group.
     Can be discussed.   Requires a majority vote.
     Can be amended.   Can be reconsidered.
6.   Amend – to change or modify the main motion (by deletion, addition, insertion, substitution.)
     Can be discussed when motion is debatable.
     Can be amended only once.
     Requires a majority vote.
     Can be reconsidered.
7.   Postpone indefinitely – to kill a motion.
     Can be discussed.
     Cannot be amended.
     Requires a majority vote.
     Only affirmative vote can be reconsidered.

All incidental motions: *deal with questions of procedure regarding pending motions.*

Have precedence over motion to which they pertain.
Arise out of immediate business at hand.
Have no definite rules of precedence among themselves.
Examples of incidental motions:
1.   Suspend a rule temporarily, change order of business.
2.   Close or reopen nominations.
3.   Withdraw a motion – the second need not consent, consent of the assembly is needed.
4.   Rise to point of order or question – call attention to procedure, or seek clarification.
5.   Division of the question – to consider by paragraph.
6.   Division of the assembly – call for a doubtful vote to be taken again.
7.   Appeal from decision of chair – must be made immediately.
8.   Object to consideration of a question.

All privileged motions: *apply to situations needing immediate attention and do not relate to the pending question.*

May interrupt other business.
Take precedence over all other motions.
Are not debatable.
Bring up urgent matters.
Examples:
1. To fix time to which to adjourn.
2. To recess.
3. To adjourn.
4. To go into executive session: only specified members/staff may attend; proceedings must be kept secret; decisions may be made public.

All unclassified motions: *cannot be made if any other motion is pending.*

Examples:
1. Take from the table, bring up a tabled motion.
2. Reconsider.
3. Rescind decision on a motion.
4. Renew.
5. Amend something already adopted.
6. Discharge a committee.
7. Ratify.

PROCEDURE FOR HANDLING A MAIN MOTION

1. **Obtain the floor:** a member rises or raises hand, waits to be recognized by the chair.
2. **Assign the floor:** the chair recognizes the member by name.
3. **State the motion:** the member introduces the business she has to offer by saying "I move that..." or "I move to..."
4. **Second the motion:** another member, without rising, says "I second the motion." When a motion comes from a committee, no second is needed (the committee members have been the seconds). If there is no second, the chair states "For want of a second, the motion is lost."
5. **Restate the motion:** after the motion is properly offered and seconded, the chair states "It is moved and seconded that..."
6. **Discuss or debate:** the chair asks "Is there any discussion?" Discussion, pro and con, follows including suggested changes and procedures (see Motions, pages 41-43).
    The maker of the motion may speak first in favor of the motion.
7. **Vote on the question** (see VOTING page 47): the chair restates the motion ("puts the question"), then says "Those in favor of the motion will signify by saying 'aye'." (Members respond.) "Those opposed, will say 'no'." (Members respond.)
8. **Announce the result of the vote:** the chair states "The ayes have it – the motion is carried," or "The noes have it – the motion is lost." A tie vote is lost, but the presiding officer may vote to break a tie.

GENERAL RULES OF DEBATE

1. The presiding officer should be addressed by title: "Madam President," or "Mr. Chairman."
2. The presiding officer should speak in the third person as: "The Chair rules…"
3. A member must be recognized in order to speak.
4. Only one main motion may be considered at a time, and must be disposed of before a new main motion may be considered, although certain subsidiary, privileged and incidental motions are in order (see page 41-43).
5. All questions must be directed to or through the chair: "Madam President, would the previous speaker explain….?"
6. The maker of a motion may speak first in debate, may not <u>speak</u> against the motion but may <u>vote</u> against it.
7. A member may not speak too long, more than 10 minutes, or more than twice on the same day to the same motion; no member should speak the second time as long as any other member who has not spoken wishes to speak.
8. Members should observe rules of courtesy, avoid references to personality and motive, and speak only to the business at hand.
9. The chair should attempt to balance speakers for and against a motion, may deliberately ask for pro and con.
10. After a question has been acted on, it can only be brought up again at the same meeting by reconsideration of the vote that disposed of it or, if tabled, by being taken from the table.

ROLE OF PARTICIPANTS IN A MEETING

1. Arrive on time, stay through the meeting.
2. Understand the purposes, goals of the meeting.
3. Ask questions for clarification.
4. Come prepared as needed.
5. Share information, talents, expertise.
6. Be receptive, open-minded and courteous.
7. Avoid private conversations.
8. Cooperate to make decisions, solve problems.
9. Express opinions, make motions, take part in debate, vote.
10. Support the policies, decisions and activities of the group, when decided democratically by the majority.

THE FEDERATION OF
JEWISH WOMEN'S
ORGANIZATIONS
OF MARYLAND

Founded in 1916,
the Federation of Jewish
Women's Organizations
of Maryland
Is an umbrella group of
non-profit organizations and
sisterhoods committed to
leadership training, support
of the Jewish community
and advocacy
of issues of major concern.

Federation is:

- The voice of over 5000 Jewish women
- The representative to community and government officials
- The venue to share and collaborate among Jewish women's groups

Federation provides:

- Leadership training and *Leadership Logic*
- Networking opportunities
- Educational & informative programs
- Calendar of events of organizations
- Annual resolutions on issues of concern
- Newsletter—*The Flame*
- Holiday supplies to members of US armed services

Website:
jewishwomensfed.org
Email:
info@jewishwomensfed.org

VOTING

Voting is the formal expression of opinion to designate approval or rejection of a proposal.

Methods of voting

1. General consent: when it is apparent that all approve, the chair states "If there are no objections,…." (If there is any objection, the matter must be put to vote.)
2. Voice vote: aye or no.
3. Show of hands: for or against.
4. Rising vote: for or against.
5. Ballot: a written vote to assure voter's secrecy.
6. Roll call: records attendance as well as vote.
7. Mail, proxy, telephone votes by conference call, or electronic voting by e-mail or fax may be used only when specified in bylaws; these provide for absentee voting.
   - A proxy is the power of attorney given by a person entitled to vote to another (a designated person) to allow that second person to vote in the place of the first.

Size of vote

1. Majority: more than half of votes cast by persons entitled to vote.
2. Plurality: the largest number of votes cast by persons entitled to vote.
3. A 2/3 vote: requires the vote by persons (entitled to vote) cast FOR to be twice as large as the vote cast AGAINST.
4. Unanimous vote: when every member voting votes the same way.
5. Tie vote: an equal number of votes cast for and against; the chair may vote to make or break a tie.
6. When a vote is in question, a member may move, or the presiding officer may call for, another vote by actual count: a show of hands or a rising vote for members to count off, a row at a time, then be seated.

USING PARLIAMENTARY PROCEDURE

To help pass motions		To help defeat motions	
1.	Second the motion.	1.	Do not second the motion.
2.	Speak FOR the motion.	2.	Speak AGAINST the motion.
3.	Vote FOR the motion.	3.	Vote AGAINST the motion.
4.	Propose meaningful amendments.	4.	Move to postpone a decision.
5.	Defeat adverse amendments.	5.	Move to table the motion.
6.	Defeat previous question to continue discussion.	6.	Move previous question to close discusion.
7.	Move for recess to influence voters, or move to refer to a committee for further study.	7.	Move for recess to influence voters, or for further study.
8.	Move to postpone to a specific time, to influence voters and for increased attendance.	8.	Move to postpone to a specific time, to influence voters and for increased attendance.
9.	Help execute passed motions to prevent motions to rescind or reconsider.	9.	If motion passes, move to reconsider; if motion passes, but is not executed, move to rescind at next meeting.

Be sure to vote – every vote counts.

An abstention is not a vote and is not recorded unless requested by the non-voter.

Based on tactics in <u>Demeter's Manual of Parliamentary Law</u>, Little Brown & Co.

PROGRAMMING

Programming is the sum total of all the meetings, projects and activities of the organization; effective programming includes well-planned business meetings and informative, stimulating and/or entertainming programs and events.

Purposes
1. To communicate and further the organization's goals, purposes, activities and concerns; goals may be long or short range.
   - Long range goals are the ongoing education and involvement of members working to accomplish the group's mission.
   - A short range goal may be fundraising for a specific project.
2. To respond to membership needs and desires, considering: age, educational levels, talents, interests, concerns, expectations, time available and geographic distances.
3. To create committed, concerned, involved members through programming that educates, enriches, influences, inspires, motivates, persuades, stimulates and satisfies.
4. To act as a showcase to project the organization's image.

THE PROGRAM COMMITTEE

Personnel
1. Chairman plus one or more co-chairmen, or vice-chairmen.
2. President or vice-president in charge.
3. Members who will chair individual meetings during the year.
4. Members with varied interests and experience, ideas and creativity, former chairmen.
5. Chairmen of other related committees involved, such as publicity, arrangements, refreshments, decorations, education, etc.

Responsibilities of the Program Chairman
1. Learn budget allocations (for expenses) and budget expectations (for fundraisers).
2. Schedule, call and preside at meetings of the committee; keep records (minutes and file of relevant materials).
3. Assign and coordinate responsibilities for each segment of the program; should be affordable, attractive, appropriate.
   - Format: speaker, film, skit, trip, etc.

- Publicity.
- Physical arrangements.
- Refreshments.
- Decorations, displays, etc.
4. Consult with the president, as to agenda and time allotted.
5. Arrange for appropriate publicity.
6. Coordinate arrangements for refreshments and clean up.
7. Prepare opening and closing remarks for the program portion of the meeting; include proper acknowledgements.
8. On the program date:
   - Check all physical facilities: microphones, lighting, ventilation, seating arrangements, props, water for speakers, etc.
   - Observe guest/speaker protocol (see pages 59, 71-78).
   - Introduce the program with enthusiasm and brevity.
9. Follow-up activities:
   - Write thank you note(s) to all involved.
   - Submit vouchers for expenses.
   - Hold evaluation session(s) with committee members.
   - Prepare and present committee report to the board and/or the membership.

Committee procedures

1. Coordinate, plan programs that provide a year's well-rounded and varied offerings that are compatible with the group's mission.
   - Establish regular meeting dates, if possible.
   - Work within budget allotments and expectations; observe realistic financial planning.
   - Respect local organization calendar as well as school, religious, and civic holidays.
2. Consider all possible formats and resources.
3. Contact speakers, preview films, rehearse skits, meet with panelists, etc. for timing, coverage of subject, physical arrangements needed, etc.
   - Use official stationery; state purpose of organization.
   - Specify exact date, time and place; confirm phone conversations in writing.
   - Secure background and/or biographical information and photographs for purposes of publicity, introductions, credits.
   - Arrange transportation, meeting of guests/speakers, diet restrictions; receiving and handling of films or slides, printed or other materials.

4.   Divide responsibilities, provide for coordination of details and timetable for each task.

PROJECTS AND ACTIVITIES

Purposes
1.   To further the organization's missions/goals.
2.   To involve membership in meaningful ways – through committee planning and individual services.
3.   To respond to members' interests, needs and desires.
4.   To create awareness, commitment, concern, involvement of members in humanitarian and community causes.
5.   To enhance the quality of community life.
6.   To present a positive image of the organization.
7.   To create pride of members in identification with group and its accomplishments.

Choosing projects
1.   Service and fund-raising efforts which further the group's mission and purposes.
   - Adjuncts/auxiliaries of established institutions – health care, educational, religious, cultural institutions.
   - Education, fund-raising to support the organization itself – lectures, study groups, gift shops, boutiques, trips, publications, etc.
2.   Support of humanitarian and community causes
   - Health, educational services.
   - Hunger, homeless, literacy needs.
   - Community and health fund drives
   - Arts, cultural, educational, penal institutions.
   - Local, national, international concerns and issues. (also see Advocacy and Action (pages 81-83).
3.   Working with community agencies and institutions as interested partners
   - Identify genuine needs
   - Become familiar with the purposes, leadership and clientele.
   - Report progress and activities of project(s) to board and membership.
   - Publicize organization's involvement in the community.

Suggested membership activities

1. Special interest groups
   - Educational, study classes, book reviews, reading clubs, language classes.
   - Youth, senior citizen, singles, single parent, bereavement support.
   - Contact with "home-bound" members.
   - Skills development: leadership, music, choral groups.
   - Arts and crafts, sewing, cooking for pleasure and/or for fundraising.
   - Tours and trips.
   - Health screening, fitness programs.
   - Hobbies – bridge, dance, art classes, exhibits, competition.
2. Intergenerational, family events/programs.
3. Holiday observances.

FUNDRAISING

Need for funds

- Administrative: operating costs, services to members.
- Programming: meetings, activities.
- Continuing or special projects.
- Philanthropies: general contributions, community causes, institutional support.

Potential sources of income

- Dues: annual dues, classes of membership.
- Assessments for special purposes.
- Registration and admission fees.
- Collections at meetings.
- Tuition: study groups, classes, self-improvement courses.
- Sales: home-made items; boutiques; commercial items such as candy, pocketbooks, jewelry, stationery, flowers, photographs, magazine subscriptions; items on consignment; nearly-new sales.

- Insurance, credit card plans
- Contributions: to general and/or special funds through memorial or special occasion cards
- Special fundraising events: donors, dances, suppers, concerts, theater parties, trips, bazaars, auctions, etc.
- Annual giving campaigns – solicitations of members.
- Publications: manuals, ad books, cookbooks, membership rosters, holiday greetings, memorial books, tribute journals, organization calendars.
- Selling services: baby-sitting, car washing, catering, etc.
- Establishment of endowment funds to provide monies for facilities management and maintenance; investment income used for repair, replacement, renovation and future needs.
- Planning giving: naming opportunities – facilities, plaques, bequests, legacies, annuities, endowments, scholarships.
- Foundations, corporate contributions.
- Government grants, allowances.

Checklist for choosing philanthropic projects and membership activities

- Is this a genuine need? Is the need well-defined?
- Does the project contribute to organization's purposes?
- Does the community need match the interests, concerns, abilities of members?
- Can the project fit into the overall programming schedule of the organization and its members?
- Can the project be accomplished by the group in terms of time, effort, personnel, anticipated profit?
- Will the results be commensurate with the time, effort and funds expended?
- Will the involvement in and the accomplishment of the project enhance the members' pride in the group, the group's public image?
- Will the cause appeal to members so that they will support it with time, effort, funds and enthusiasm?
- Are the stated goals realistic? Is there a stated goal?
- Is training or orientation needed by individuals involved? Are they willing and able? Advisable to retain a consultant?

THE SPECIAL FUNDRAISING EVENT

General Committee Procedures
- Name specific purpose(s) for the funds.
- Determine the amount of funds needed; be realistic in budgeting.
- Select the type of fundraiser.
- Choose the date: clear with community and holiday calendars; check dates of sports events, community drives; investigate possibility of combining with another group.
- Involve members in decision-making, planning and implementing; large working committees give many people a stake in the success of the affair.
- Evaluate the procedures and results.

Suggested special events: be sure to check legal aspects such as licenses; admissions and other taxes, exemptions, mailing regulations, etc.
- Sales: auctions, "nearly new" sales, flea markets, garage sales, antique shows, swap shops, bazaars, home-made goods, gift shops, boutique items, country stores, book fairs.
- Testimonial affairs: to honor a member or members, a community personality; a memorial in honor of an individual or event.
- Donor affairs: pay-as-you-go, earn-your-donor, fill-a-blank, pledge card, single payment, donor plus admission or donor to include admission.
- Social events: card parties, dances, covered dish suppers, progressive dinners.
- Entertainment: lectures, entertainers, well-known personalities, fashion shows, repertory groups, home talent, theater parties; sports events.
- Exhibits: art, antique, hobby shows; demonstrations.
- Trips and tours: house and garden, museums, historic buildings, pilgrimages, vacations, theater trips, charters.
- Publications: ad books, cookbooks, histories, anniversary editions, postcards, memorial plates or plaques.
- Discount and credit programs in cooperation with merchants, theaters, trading stamp companies.

Publicity/Marketing for special events (see Publicity, pages 66-70)
- Plan a campaign, with a theme and a logo, step-by-step, up to the date, and follow-up afterward ("thank you" or "we missed you").

- Create enthusiasm; make people want to give, to attend; aim for publicity to be striking, but appropriate and in good taste.
- Use various means of publicity: newspapers, radio, TV, internet, mailings, throw-aways, posters, enthusiastic members, etc.
- Use personal solicitation for patronage, ticket sales.
- Sell the cause and the organization as well as the event.

SUGGESTED PROGRAM AIDS

Resources
- Membership: talents, experiences, expertise.
- Health, education, welfare, social agencies and institutions.
- Government agencies and departments: local, state and federal.
- Schools, universities
- Art galleries, museums, libraries, historical societies.
- Theater, dance, music groups; symphony, ballet, opera companies.
- Communications media: radio, TV, newspapers, magazines, internet.
- Ecumenical, religious, ethnic groups.
- Civic leaders, judges, elected officials.
- Philanthropic, fraternal organizations.
- Human relations, social action, consumer groups.
- Business, professional, trade associations; investment, estate planners.
- Travel agents, travelers.
- Speakers' bureaus, theatrical agents and agencies.
- Local, regional, national organizations with like aims.
- The organization's parent body or affiliated groups.
- Books and publications; authors.

Formats
- Speaker; speaker plus discussion, buzz sessions, films, slides, demonstrations.
- Panel, symposium, forum; debate, structured debate.
- Dialogue; question and answer session(s).
- Interview; taped, recorded interviews.

- Role-playing, socio-drama plus speaker, discussion or buzz sessions.
- Workshops, seminars, problem clinics, think-tank sessions.
- Film, slide, tape, record, multimedia presentations.
- Film, music, dance, art festivals.
- Book fairs, autograph parties.
- Book review, book review plus reading or dramatic presentation.
- Dramatizations, skits, shows; living history, living legends.
- Adaptations of radio, TV shows or scripts.
- Games, quizzes, contests.
- Exhibits, expositions.
- Demonstrations, "how-to" or "do-it-yourself" sessions; crafts, decorations, bake-in, sew-in, paint-in, etc.
- Bazaars, sales, auctions.
- Classes, study groups, courses of single or several sessions.
- Field trips, tours, excursions, sports events.

CONVENTION PLANNING

A convention is an assembly of designated delegates or representatives of chapters or local groups meeting together to transact the business of an umbrella or parent organization.

Bylaws requirements

1. Establish schedule for holding periodic conventions.
2. Specify qualifications, number of delegates and how chosen.
3. Define voting members and quorum, nomination and election procedures.

Formal organization

1. Opening ceremonies and welcome: may be inspirational, not regarded as business.
2. Call to order by presiding officer to open the business meeting.
3. Special convention committees.

a. Credentials Committee:
- Distributes the "call to convention" together with credential forms to be returned by a specific date.
- Arranges for registration of delegates and identification badges.
- Prepares and presents its report at the opening meeting, supplementary reports at first meeting each day and final report at last meeting.

b. Committee on Standing Rules:
- Proposes procedures as "special rules of order" to expedite business.
- Includes rules as part of "packet" of information distributed at registration.
- States method of introducing resolutions, if not specified in bylaws.

c. Program Committee:
- Plans schedule and titles of workshops, special events, speakers, etc. to cover all aspects of the organization's activities.
- Works closely with an Arrangements Committee, which plans room assignments, reservations, meals, seating, transportation, etc., including tax deductible information.
- Prepares preliminary schedule to be mailed to each constituent group and/or delegate prior to convention.
- Distributes a final, printed schedule to each delegate in a convention packet at registration.
- Announces general program format at opening meeting.
- Provides evaluation forms to be filled out by delegates at convention's end.

d. Resolutions Committee
- Drafts and sends proposed resolutions to delegates in advance.
- Presents resolutions to the convention for action.

Election of officers at a convention
1. Usually takes place before the final meeting, installation at the final meeting.

Professional staff works closely with officers and committees to coordinate all details.

HOW TO BE AN EFFECTIVE DELEGATE

A delegate is a person sent to a conference or convention as the representative of an organization to meet together with others due to common purposes, activities and interests.

Qualifications of a delegate

1. Commitment to and understanding of the local organization's goals and activities, its relationship to the larger assembly.
2. Understanding of the purposes of the larger group and its relationship to the local organization.
3. Ability to interpret goals, activities and projects of both the local and the larger group.
4. Willingness to attend the convention and become familiar with the agenda and issues <u>beforehand.</u>
5. Open-mindedness; willingness to learn and broaden horizons.

Responsibilities of a delegate

1. To the conference/convention
   - Do homework: read materials; become familiar with the issues and programs on the convention agenda.
   - Know the local organization's reaction or position on each issue to come before the convention/conference.
   - Be prepared to voice the local organization's viewpoint.
   - Attend all sessions.
   - Participate fully: share ideas; compare techniques; listen and take notes; enter discussions; ask questions.
   - Gather information, materials for local use.
2. To the local organization
   - Represent the organization's goals and viewpoints.
   - Prepare written or oral reports as requested; include program highlights, action taken, personal reaction.
   - Share, disseminate, interpret information and materials gathered.
   - Refer specific suggestions, ideas, techniques to the president and appropriate officers and committees for consideration.
3. Voting
   - The <u>instructed</u> delegate: when the local organization has taken a position on an issue to come before the conven-

tion, the instructed delegate must vote that position at the convention.

- The <u>informed</u>, but uninstructed delegate: if, while the convention is in session, changes are made during the presentation or discussion of an issue on which the local organization has taken a position, the delegate votes using discretion and judgement, based on knowledge of the position taken by the local group and the degree or type of changes proposed.

GUEST PROTOCOL

Organizational protocol refers to procedures which are deemed correct and courteous and are observed according to precedent and established etiquette.

Prior to the meeting

1. Invitation to bring greetings, as speaker, as honoree.
   - Offer choice of dates, if possible.
   - Send invitation in writing on official stationery, reason for invitation.
   - Write confirmation if initial contact was by phone.
   - Inquire as to fee or honorarium.
   - Specify date, time, place; size, purpose, mission of organization; time allotted, function on program.
   - Inquire as to mode of travel, arrival and departure times.
   - Send copies of announcements/invitations, publicity, etc.
2. Guest welfare
   - Arrange to meet guest(s).
   - Ask permission to schedule extra events such as reception, press or TV interview.
   - Provide schedule of events, agenda.
   - Plan for overnight accommodations, if necessary; arrange direct payment.
   - Pay for meals, provide tickets as necessary.

At the meeting

1. Arrange to greet guest at door, if not escorted to meeting; assign someone to accompany guest until meeting begins.
2. Explain program of the day, guest's place on program.
3. Check platform arrangements and props with guest.
4. Observe seating protocol:
   - Presiding officer in center; introduces people at head table(s).
   - Guest of honor at right of presiding officer.
   - Additional guests interspersed among officers.
5. Provide place cards at head table.
6. Adhere to time schedule.
7. Give short, gracious introduction(s); pronounce name(s) correctly.
8. Express thanks sincerely after the guest speaks; president adjourns the meeting.
9. Have honorarium or gift ready for speaker/guest.
10. Arrange for guest to be escorted to the door or to transportation.

Following the meeting

1. Send thank-you note(s) promptly.
2. Send copies of follow-up publicity, if any.
3. Schedule an evaluation of the meeting/event.

ADDRESSING PERSONS IN OFFICIAL POSITIONS

OFFICIAL	ADDRESS	SALUTATION
The President	The President The White House Washington, D.C. 20500	Mr. President:
The Vice President	The Vice President The United States Senate Washington, D.C. 20510	Mr. Vice-President:
Justices of the Supreme Court	The Honorable_____, Chief Justice or Associate Justice U.S. Supreme Court Washington, D.C. 20543	Dear Mr. Justice_____:
United States Senator	The Honorable_____ Senate Office Building Washington, D.C. 20510	Dear Senator_____:
United States Representative	The Honorable_____ House of Representatives Washington, D.C. 20515	Dear Representative _____:
United States Cabinet Secretary	The Honorable_____, Secretary of _____ Department of _____	Dear Secretary_____:
U.S. Mission to the United Nations	The Honorable_____ U.S. Mission to the U.N. 799 United Nations Plaza New York, New York 10017	Dear _____:
Governor	The Honorable (John Smith), State Capitol	Dear Governor_____:
Mayor	His Honor Mayor (John Smith), City Hall	Dear Mayor _____:

OFFICIAL	ADDRESS	SALUTATION
Cardinal	His Eminence (John) Cardinal (Smith), Archbishop of _____	Your Eminence: or Dear Cardinal_____:
Archbishop	The Most Reverend (John Smith), Archbishop of _____	Your Excellency: or Dear Archbishop_____:
Priest	The Reverend Father (John Smith), Church of _____	Dear Father _____:
Nun	Sister_____, (order) (address) _____	Dear Sister_____:
Minister	The Reverend (John Smith), Church of _____	Dear Reverend_____:
Rabbi	Rabbi (John Smith), or Dr. _____ (if holding a degree) Congregation _____	Dear Rabbi (Smith): or Dr._____:

FLAG AND ANTHEM PROTOCOL

Flags
1. Other nation's flags may be displayed with the American flag.
2. U.S. flag is put in position first.
3. Flags should be the same size.
4. U.S. flag should be on speaker's right on a dais.
5. Flags of other nations are placed on speaker's left on a dais.
6. U.S. flag is placed to the right of the audience on an auditorium floor.
7. When the U.S. flag is hung on a wall (like a banner), the field of stars is on the upper left of the person(s) facing it.

Anthems
1. The Star Spangled Banner is played <u>after</u> the foreign country's anthem, even when the guest speaker or foreign dignitary is from that nation.
2. When a visiting performer or group (foreign chorus or orchestra) performs the two anthems, the anthem of the visiting group's country is played last.

Information from Fort McHenry National Monumen t and Historic Site.

PUBLIC RELATIONS – PUBLICITY
MARKETING – IMAGE BUILDING

Public Relations is the influencing of public opinion through communication; good public relations establish rapport and promote goodwill. Publicity is communication through the preparation and distribution of information; to be effective, it should have news value and generate interest. Marketing is the process of advertising and selling a product: a cause, an event, an organization.

Purposes

1. To develop and promote awareness of the organization's mission and goals.
2. To publicize the activities of the organization in order to encourage members and potential members to participate in those activities.
3. To increase and diversify membership, attendance, support; to target specific audiences.
4. To create a good public image, public understanding, support and goodwill.

Responsibilities of the publicity committee

1. Be aware of public relations value of all communications; recognize the importance of promoting the organization: its purposes, activities, accomplishments, members, newsworthiness.
2. Communicate the organization's message, verbally and in writing.
3. Contact the news media; learn and observe deadlines and preparation of material required; be courteous, cooperative and conscientious.
4. Make all publicity interesting, accurate, attractive and easy to understand.

General Procedures

1. Consult with president and other committees in planning over-all publicity well in advance, including a calendar of mailing dates.
2. Investigate budgetary allotments, financial limitations and facilities available.
3. Check postal regulations, rates, and eligibility for non-profit permit.

4. Establish needs for publicity and the methods to be used: direct mail, news media, paid advertisements, verbal announcements, e-mail, etc.

5. Learn about printing processes; if to be done professionally, get bids; choose the processes that meet the needs and budget; tailor material to suite the process: mimeograph, multilith, offset, letterpress, electrostencil, lithograph, copy machines, desktop publishing, computer technology.

6. Develop and keep mailing lists up-to-date (members, prospective members, community calendars, etc.).

7. Make personal contacts with news media personnel; learn and observe deadlines and rules in preparing releases, faxes, e-mail addresses, and web sties.

8. Always include the 5 W's:
   - WHAT organization (use full name and title of the event).
   - WHO will speak, preside, arranged the program, and is responsible.
   - WHEN the event will take place; be accurate, complete: day, date and time.
   - WHERE the event will take place; where to get more information.
   - WHY the event is being held; regular, special meeting, fundraising.

9. Keep complete file of all publicity, newsletters, flyers, announcements, newspaper clippings, correspondence (including e-mail), etc.

INTERNAL PUBLICITY

Internal publicity includes any communication directed to members and supporters. It includes correspondence, membership directories, displays prepared for meetings as well as periodicals, publications and announcements.

Publications: bulletins, newsletters, brochures, flyers and posters
1. Meeting notices, announcements of current, future events.
2. Calendar of events.
3. Committee activities and personnel.
4. Lists of new members, newly elected officers.
5. Feature stories about members.
6. Articles of general information pertinent to the organization's goals and interests.
7. Reports of participation in community affairs; attendance and reports of delegates at conferences.
8. Items inviting comments.
9. Reviews of previous meetings, completed projects.
10. Annual reports.

Procedures
1. Secure competent editorial committee: editor, reporters, art editor, production crew for typing, addressing, etc.
2. Provide a realistic budget allowance for printing and postage.
3. Keep the editor informed with a master calendar of events, committee reports, policy decisions, etc.
4. Create a distinctive "trade mark," logo, or masthead; use it consistently.
5. Plan an attractive format, professional in appearance: eye-catching, easy-to-read articles; solid type is uninteresting; use figures, space, "boxes," pictures, subtitles and varied type.
6. Prepare rough drafts, revise, edit; digest news, paying particular attention to the 5 W's: who, what, where, when, why and how.
7. Proof read for accuracy.
8. Don't assume the reader knows: goal is to give information, to stimulate, motivate the reader-member to attend, to support.
9. Send issues to special guests or groups that have received recognition in the publication; include parent body on regular mailing list.

10. Develop a marketing strategy: written and visual communications; target audiences.

EXTERNAL PUBLICITY

External publicity refers to communications and advertisements about the organization that are directed outside the membership.

Newspapers: daily, weekly, etc. (see Appendix VI., sample release)
1. Know what is newsworthy:
   - Meeting, program, project announcements.
   - Fundraising events, purposes of funds.
   - Election, installation of officers.
   - Appointment of committees, committee chairmen.
   - Accomplishments of the group, of individual members.
   - Awards presented to the group, by the group.
   - Special occasions: anniversaries, dedications.
   - Membership campaigns.
   - Community services: initiated, ongoing, completed, sponsored.
   - Cooperation, participation in community affairs.
   - Group action taken, stands made.
   - Members' attendance at conferences.
   - Special guests, visitors.
   - Follow-up reports after special events.
2. Become familiar with the newspapers: format, style, regular and special features, deadlines, policies; learn names of editors, heads of departments.
3. Use various departments of the paper:
   - Club editor for regular meetings, election information, etc.
   - Sports editor for athletic events.
   - Arts editor for concerts, exhibits, films, etc.
   - Real estate for new building or relocation of office.
   - Education editor for seminars, how-to publications, etc.
   - Columnists, feature editors for human interest stories,

awards, personalities; contributions or sponsorships of funds, equipment, community services, etc.

- News editors for emergency services offered or performed.
- Book editor for new or revised publications, book reviews, book fairs.
- Classified section for paid announcements.
- Consumer affairs editor for related information.
- Letters to the editor concerning a current issue or statement.

4. Preparing the newspaper release.
- Send release in compliance with deadlines to specific department/editor.
- Use "news" style: include the 5 W's in first part of the story; if story is cut, the essential information will still be there.
- Be absolutely accurate in spelling of names, use of titles.
- Use short words, short sentences, and short paragraphs.
- Thank editors for their cooperation, courtesy.
- Type story – double-spaced on standard size 8 1/2" x 11" paper; use one side only.
    - Start typing about halfway down the page to leave room for headline to be added; leave 1 1/2" margins on both right and left sides.
    - In upper left-hand corner type source information: name of organization, address and phone number of writer or organization for verification.
    - In upper right-hand corner type requested date for appearance of the story: FOR RELEASE-DATE.
    - Keep copy of each release in case verification is needed.
    - Make an original for each editor to whom the release is sent; do not send copies, handwritten copy, duplicate copies.
    - Copy should be brief; if a second page is necessary, end the page with a complete paragraph; indicate MORE at the bottom of the first page; number and head each page.
    - Indicate the end of the article in some way as: -30-; -XXX-; -###-.

5. Using photographs
- Tie picture to the story; use newsworthy people, personalities, activities.

- Limit photographs to 3 or 4 people; arrange grouping for eye-appeal.
- Send black and white glossy prints 4" x 5", 5" x 7" or 8" x 10".
- Do note write on reverse side; type information on attached sheet.
- Provide correct names and titles of individuals photographed according to their positions in the picture.
- Do not expect the picture to be returned, unless specifically arranged for.
- Upon request, an editor may send a staff photographer to a newsworthy event: communicate the purpose, work cooperatively, courteously.

Radio and TV: spot announcements, interviews, appearances (see Appendix VI, sample release)

1. Request time only for newsworthy items: meetings, projects, accomplishments, special events, why the public may be interested.
2. Become familiar with the local station's format, timing, personnel, programs, policies; tailor announcements to these requirements.
3. State clearly the event you want publicized; include all pertinent information.
4. Research local stations for possibility of personal appearances on talk or interview shows, contests, etc; remember public service broadcast stations.
5. Establish exact times, names of interviewers, information desired, facts to be projected; know the facts.
6. Verbally and in written form, thank the interviewer or program director for time allotted, interest shown.
7. National/parent organizations often have films and spots available; arrange to have these shown locally.

Additional publicity techniques

1. Direct mailings: letters, announcements, brochures, tickets.
   - Name of organization should be prominent; use letterhead, logo, etc.
   - Tailor the mailing piece to the purpose: to inform, solicit support, express concern, urge action.
   - State subject clearly, simply in positive, straightforward manner; use attractive, easy to read style.

- Observe proper forms of address, correct titles, rules of courtesy, postal regulations.

2. Advertising specialties, attention-getters: buttons, tags, stickers, labels, sample giveaways, etc.

3. Posters, announcements in libraries, public buildings, merchants' windows, apartment houses, meeting places, community centers, community bulletin boards; always get prior consent to place them.

4. Press coverage for special events
   - Notify the media well in advance of the event and/or the appearance of a well-known personality (speaker, entertainer, guest).
   - Send photographs with news release of the event; include biographical information and significance of guest's appearance.
   - Contact the appropriate newspaper editor, radio or TV program director for assignment of a staff reporter or photographer to cover the event.
   - Arrange for press conference(s), interview(s), photograph session(s) with the media and the guest.
   - Invite the press to the event; provide seating and complimentary tickets.

5. Street banners, billboards, signs; get permission from city authorities, observe zoning laws.

6. Ad books, program books, paid advertisements.

7. Awards, tributes, honors, prizes, trophies, certificates.

8. Personal contacts: telephone calls; letters.

9. Display, information booths; bulletin boards.

SPEAKING IN PUBLIC

Speaking in public may range from a simple welcome or announcement to a formal lecture or emotional appeal for a worthy cause.
Public speaking is a form of communication that influences thinking or behavior; molds opinion; educates or informs; generates discussion, action, interaction.
The basic elements to be considered and general procedures remain the same, whether making a brief announcement or delivering a formal address.

The audience

1. Who: name of group and its purpose; ages, interests, size of group, prior knowledge of subject, relationship to speaker.
2. What: kind of group – intimate gathering or mass meeting committee, board or general meeting of an organization.
3. Why: purpose of meeting – to plan, decide, act; for inspiration, information, motivation, etc.
4. When, where: time and place, length of meeting, overall agenda.

The speech

1. Preparation: think, consult, research, organize; outline or write out important details; KNOW YOUR SUBJECT.
2. Practice: time yourself, speaking aloud before a mirror or with a tape recorder; watch, emulate those you admire; avoid faults you dislike in others.
3. Presentation: dress comfortably; arrive early; follow platform etiquette; wait for attention, pause, address group; show sincerity, conviction; be concise, relevant, courteous; concentrate on the speech, not yourself; don't memorize – speak from an outline or written text, whichever is easier; use simple language; define when necessary; avoid abstractions, cliches; use specific examples where possible, humor if it comes naturally.

The speaker

1. Posture: sit and stand tall; look alert and interested; enter and leave easily and quietly; rest hands comfortably, feet slightly apart; good posture inspires respect and confidence.
2. Facial expressions and gestures convey feelings; smile pleasantly; gesture only if it comes naturally.

3. Voice: tone conveys attitude; speak clearly, enunciate; pronounce names correctly; project without shouting; use pauses for emphasis; vary rhythm and voice intensity.
4. Self-improvement.
   - Use books, tapes, films.
   - Enroll in courses through schools, colleges, self-help programs.
   - Study, learn from effective speakers.
   - Evaluate yourself; be honest with self-criticism.

OCCASIONS FOR SPEAKING IN PUBLIC

The welcome
1.　　Sets the tone for whatever is to follow.
2.　　An act of friendliness: feel friendly; convey warmth, sincerity.

Invocations and benedictions
1.　　Purpose: to invoke blessing on the assembly and its work.
2.　　Choosing the person.
- Clergy, special guest.
- Designation of a chaplain by the group.
- Choice of a member as an honor, sufficient prior notice having been given.
3.　　Preparation.
- An established prayer from liturgy or another well-known source; the group's own prayer or creed; an original prayer written for the occasion.
- Suitability: for the occasion, group, season, etc.
- Content: may combine various aspects of prayer as praise, thanksgiving, petition, aspiration.
4.　　Presentation
- Stand before the group; invite the group to stand.
- Pause for silence.
- Speak clearly, audibly, reverently.
- Invite participation if a familiar prayer is used.
- After closing words, pause a moment, then be seated.

Greetings (as a guest)
1.　　Preparation: know the correct name of the group, its purposes, achievements, the formality or informality of the occasion.
2.　　Presentation
- Stand, address by name or office the individual who welcomes or introduces you.
- Smile; use warm, friendly tone.
- Convey greetings in the name of the group you represent.
- Be brief; acknowledge reason for being present, gratitude for personal courtesies; compliment the group and wish it continued success.

Awards and acceptances
1.   Purpose
- Presentation of a gift or honor: the gift is merely a symbol; the <u>reason</u> for giving it is essential.
- Acceptance of a gift or honor completes the act of presentation, allows for expression of gratitude.

2.   Preparation
- Research the history of the gift, its importance, who previous recipients have been.
- Learn pertinent facts about the person receiving it.
- Plan the actual physical presentation.

3.   Presentation
- Stand before the group to get attention.
- Use warm, friendly tone; show admiration and respect without being overlavish in praise.
- Include occasion for the award, background information, the gift itself (may display it at this time).
- If the recipient has not been announced, build up suspense; mention name last.
- Give pertinent information about the recipient, using correct title and pronunciation of name.
- Present gift or award at end of remarks.

4.   Acceptance
- Be natural; don't rush forward.
- Be sure to hold up gift for all to see.
- Be simple, sincere, brief.
- Concentrate on your feelings: gratitude, pride, satisfaction, etc.
- Mention the value you place on the gift, and the group presenting it.
- Name others involved, if you accept for a group or have been part of a group.
- Mention thanks once again; shake hands if it is natural to do so; be seated.

Announcements and reports
1.   Purpose: to arouse interest, give information, move to action.
2.   Preparation
- Have information written and at hand: what, when, where, why, who and how.
- Anticipate questions that will be asked; have answers ready.

- Have written copy of report ready to give secretary for inclusion in minutes.
3. Presentation
    - Stand before the group to get attention.
    - Opening statement and convincing tone are important.
    - Speak distinctly, audibly; pronounce names and places correctly, time and amounts (such as prices) carefully.
    - Check with presiding officer or person in charge for permission to speak, for inclusion on the agenda.
    - Know material thoroughly; present it enthusiastically.
    - Repeat most important facts at the end (as date and time of event).

Introductions
1. Purpose
    - To present a guest, speaker or well-known personality.
    - To alert the group to the special characteristics and/or qualification of the individual and the message.
2. Preparation
    - Obtain biographical information; learn and use only pertinent facts.
    - Practice correct pronunciation of person's name; use correct title.
3. Presentation
    - Stand, address the group.
    - Express pleasure at guest's or speaker's presence.
    - Mention some personal tie, if appropriate.
    - Be brief, concise, relevant; this is the introduction, not the speech.
    - Stress individual's special qualifications, accomplishments or experiences that relate to the present occasion or task.
    - If a question period will follow, inform the audience at this time.
    - Lead up to the speaker's topic or guest's message: mention the title or topic, the speaker's name last as the signal to come forward.
        - When introducing a panel and moderator, introduce the topic and moderator; the moderator will introduce members of the panel.
        - When introducing members of a panel, or speakers who will follow each other, make all the introductions at once so the various points of view will follow naturally.

- Be seated and remain attentive during the presentation.
- After the speech, express thanks on behalf of the group for the message, challenge, presentation, etc.; make it pertinent, show that you were listening.
- If questions have been invited, serve as moderator.
  - Be prepared with a question.
  - Invite questions from the group.
  - Repeat each question or ask the speaker to do so, so that all can follow easily.
  - Watch the time; control the situation.
  - Thank the group.
  - Thank the speaker once again.
- The presiding officer adjourns the meeting.

Installations

1. Purpose
   - Provide for transition and continuity from one leadership group to another.
   - Allow for official and public recognition of jobs well done.
   - Present newly elected leadership to the membership.
   - Set forth duties and responsibilities of each office, be succinct.
   - Focus on the goals and purposes of the organization itself; inspire and revitalize leaders and members.
   - Offer an opportunity to honor a past president, a regional or national representative by having that person serve as installing officer.
2. Preparation
   - Invite installing officer several months in advance.
   - Use an established or prescribed installation, or prepare an original one.
   - Know the organization, its purposes and goals, its habits of formality or informality, etc.
   - Obtain relevant background information about individuals to be retired and installed.
3. The installation ceremony: according to organization's customs; samples may be obtained from books or local, regional, national organizations.
   - Address the membership, referring to accomplishments of the group.
   - Discharge officers and board members whose terms are

ending with thanks for their sincerity, dedication, jobs well done.

- Install newly elected officers with reference to their leadership responsibilities and duties.
- Present or make arrangements for retiring and new presidents to receive symbols of office (gavel, pin, etc.).
- Shake hands, be seated, as newly installed president makes speech of acceptance.

THE PUBLIC SPEECH

Purpose

To inform, inspire, challenge, convince, persuade, motivate, stimulate, entertain.

Responsibilities of a speaker

1. Answer invitations promptly; confirm date, time, place.
2. Supply biographical information when requested.
3. Allow sufficient travel time, both arrival and departure; notify hosts.
4. Ascertain type of speech wanted and time allotted: the group usually chooses the topic, the speaker gives the title.
5. Find out about the audience and the occasion.
   - Audience: size, ages, interests, knowledge of the subject, name of the group and its purposes.
   - Occasion: formal or informal; single meeting or one of a series; regular or special meeting; single presentation or one of a panel; stimulation toward action or fund raising; special assignment such as a"key-note," kick-off or wrap-up meeting.
   - Physical arrangements: lecture hall or after dinner; indoors or out; presence or absence of steps, microphone, lectern, etc.
   - Place on the agenda: single speech or one of several; part of a business meeting or the entire program, etc.

- Appropriate dress.
6. Plan the speech; be prepared.

Preparation of speech
1. Gather background information through reading, research, interviews.
2. Select pertinent material.
3. Make an outline of the facts to be included, developing the theme logically, step by step.
4. Know the facts; be familiar enough with the material to be comfortable and able to answer questions.
5. Prepare complete opening and closing sentences, a written text if requested.
6. Be sure to number pages and type double-spaced for ease of handling.
7. Underline, mark the text for pauses and emphasis.
8. Practice the speech, giving attention to timing, pauses, pronunciation, enunciation.
9. Evaluate the speech: does it accomplish its purpose, stick to its theme, develop logically, say enough or too much?

Presentation
1. Appear appropriately dressed.
2. Acknowledge introduction: smile, give greeting with warmth, sincerity.
3. Pause, to relax physically and mentally; then begin.
4. Be yourself: speak with normal pitch in a clear, conversational tone, but a little louder than usual, i.e., project your voice.
5. Begin with a well-planned opening sentence: an interesting fact, a challenge, a question.
6. Use clear, understandable language; explain technical terms.
7. Include illustrations, quotes, anecdotes that are relevant, appropriate, clear.
8. Relate subject matter to the audience when possible.
9. Emphasize important points through the use of voice, pauses, repetition, summarizing.
10. Observe the time limit.
11. Sum up; close with an effective, concise, forceful ending.

Following the presentation
1. Express thanks verbally.
2. Send written thanks for personal courtesies.

LEADING DISCUSSIONS

The discussion leader is a facilitator whose role is to elicit response and participation from all present.

Purposes of discussion sessions
1. To share ideas, experiences, information.
2. To study issues, topics.
3. To influence, develop attitudes.
4. To determine a consensus.
5. To solve problems, make decisions.

Preparation for a discussion session
1. Have a well-defined purpose: to develop an idea or attitude, solve a problem, reach a decision.
2. Know the topic at hand: the issue, subject or problem develop a discussion plan and an approach to the topic.
3. Gather facts, background material.
4. Know the group: size, background, expertise, interests and relationship to the topic or problem at hand.
5. Appoint, or ask for a volunteer recorder.

Responsibilities of a discussion leader
1. Create a friendly, accepting atmosphere; appear relaxed, courteous; use introductions, physical arrangements to put people at ease.
2. State the questions, purposes or goals of the discussion.
3. Have pertinent facts, background information at hand.
4. Help group agree on ground rules: discussion procedures, time limits, desired results.
5. Encourage members to participate freely; handle the too verbose, too-frequent contributor with courtesy; create openings for those reluctant to speak.
6. Help members respect each others' points of view, ideas, experiences, attitudes, suggestions.
7. Lead group toward reaching conclusions, making decisions, solving problems; help members accept group decisions.
8. State the decisions, conclusions, major areas of group actions or agreement; summarize the discussion.
9. Close the meeting on time, helping the group plan for future sessions or action if necessary or desirable.

Suggested techniques for discussion leaders

1. Provide a written agenda of topics to be discussed, items to be covered or decided during the session.
2. Use blackboard or large sketchpad to frame the main questions, record ideas, summarize points.
3. Ask leading questions to focus or refocus the discussion, lead to the next step, bring out different ideas and help evaluate as discussion progresses:
   - "Has anyone additional information?"
   - "Let's have some reaction to that point/suggestion."
   - "Can you help us? You've had experience with . . ." (To encourage a timid member).
   - "That's a good question . . any comments?"
   - "That is an interesting perception/statement . . . Let's hear from someone else . . ."
   - "Are there ramifications/circumstances we haven't addressed?" "Have we covered all concerns?"
   - "The group seems to be divided; can we reach a decision, find a solution, or approach it from another angle?" "Can we hone in on a solution/decision/vote?'
   - "The majority seems to think that . . . "
4. Review and summarize to help crystallize and direct group thinking, to keep the topic in focus, to provide continuity, to help the group reach conclusions.
5. Use various group dynamics techniques such as brainstorming, role-plying, buzz sessions, etc.

Responsibility of recorders

1. Record the title, date, time, purpose of the meeting.
2. Include names of discussion leaders, presenters and attendees/participants.
3. Note topics, issues discussed and/or of particular concern.
4. Identify individuals for future leadership roles.
5. List recommendations for future sessions – positive and negative reactions.
6. Participate in the discussion when appropriate.
7. Complete your report promptly and hand it in.

ADVOCACY AND ACTION

Advocacy is the support of a person, an idea, or a position on a community concern or current issue. Action can be taken in various ways by individuals and/or organizations to promote the causes which they support: to influence public opinion, public policy and/or legislation. Action may also include advocacy for changes in the way policies and services are implemented.

Basic principles
1. Any citizen may request a member of a legislature to introduce, support or defeat a bill.
2. Every lawmaker is responsive to opinions and actions of individuals and groups.
3. Action may be taken, opinions made known, at any step in the legislative process.

The legislative process
1. A bill is introduced, given a number and assigned to a committee; public hearings may be held.
2. The bill can be "killed" in committee or can be "reported out" of committee for discussion, debate and vote of that body.
3. If a similar bill on the same topic is introduced in both houses of a bicameral legislature, a conference committee may be necessary to iron out discrepancies, reach a compromise and present a bill for vote.
4. If passed, the bill may be signed into law, vetoed or no action taken.
5. A veto may be overridden by a two-thirds vote of the legislature; if no action is taken within a specified time, the bill becomes law.

Considerations in taking group action
1. The organization: its purposes, areas of interest, bylaws and policy.
2. The membership: concerns, knowledge of the issue(s), motivation to act.
3. The issue(s): importance of being selective in choosing issues and priorities for action.
4. Timeliness of the action: current status of a bill or proposal.
5. The appropriate legislators, public officials or agencies to approach with appeals for action.

6.   As part of a larger organization (a chapter or auxiliary): ascertain policy statements and action already taken by the parent group.
7.   Awareness of other organizations with similar goals taking similar action: networking, forming or joining coalitions.

Methods of influencing individual and group action

1.   Appoint a current issues or legislative chairman to study the issues, keep membership informed.
2.   Appoint an observer to attend legislative sessions and report back.
3.   Schedule study sessions to address the issues, influence attitudes, motivate individuals, take group action.
4.   Establish lines of communication to inform, influence, motivate members: newsletters, position papers.
5.   Maintain mailing list of key people – send newsletters, announcements, media clippings.
6.   Make personal contacts: attend and/or testify at hearings; visit legislators; invite legislators, officials or community activists to address the group, tour agency facilities.
   - Plan carefully points to be made.
   - Call appointments secretary to set date and time.
   - Be prepared: have information and materials to share; know pros and cons of the issues; make your position known.
   - State your request and its likely impact on voters.
   - After visit, send thank you letter; include points covered during the meeting.
7.   Agree by majority vote to take a position on an issue.
8.   Communicate that position to influence the appropriate individuals or agencies to take the action the group has urged: letters, telegrams, petitions, postcards, phone calls, faxes, e-mail, resolutions.
   - Use correct title(s) and addresses(es).
   - State purpose in first paragraph.
   - Identify specific legislation by title and number.
   - Be direct, courteous; give key reasons for position taken.
   - Name only one issue per communication, one page only.
   - Thank legislator(s) for their attention and consideration; thank those who have support(ed) your position.

Using resolutions to influence action – (SAMPLE RESOLUTIONS – Appendix VII)

Resolutions are formal motions designed to state positions on current issues and/or to urge action in support of those positions.

1. Resolutions represent group opinion arrived at democratically by majority vote and do not imply unanimity.
2. Resolutions adopted by group action serve as policy guidelines for programming, education and other activities by the group.
3. Resolutions begin the "RESOLVED, That . . . " which replaces the "I move that . . . " to introduce a motion.
4. Resolutions often begin with a preamble to state the reason(s) for the position stated as well as the action urged, as: "Believing that . . . , the (organization) urges . . . " or "Whereas, the (organization) believes that . . .; therefore, be it RESOLVED, That . . ."
5. Report issues of special concern to members, urging them to take action personally.
6. Prepare sample letters for members to use for calls, letters, faxes, emails to appropriate officials urging them to take action.
7. Allot time at meetings for reports of action(s) taken and responses received.
8. Use the issues raised by resolutions as subject matter for programs and/or special projects.

VOLUNTEER/STAFF RELATIONSHIPS

The respective roles, responsibilities and relationships of volunteers and staff in the governance and operation of agencies, institutions and organizations need to be delineated, developed, understood and respected.

Roles and Responsibilities of Volunteers

1. The president (CEO = chief executive officer)
   a. Provide leadership as role model – commitment to the organization, its mission and activities.
   b. Preside effectively: develop timed agenda, involve others in planning, decision-making, problem solving, evaluating; provide for board orientation.
   c. Appoint committee chairmen, oversee committee activity.
   d. Recruit, develop future leadership; motivate members; share and delegate; give praise.
   e. Represent the group in the community, interpret its mission, promote a good public image.
   f. Recognize, support the executive director as the professional; communicate, consult on a regular basis.
2. The board
   a. Oversee all fiscal and legal matters, funds, assets, liabilities and facilities.
   b. Establish, monitor, modify, evaluate mission statement, long and short term goals; policies, programs, projects and services – strategic planning (see pages 86-87).
   c. Promote, support, further the group's activities and public image – individually and collectively.
   d. Provide for future leadership by motivating, involving, recognizing others, rotating board positions.
   e. Recruit, select, employ and evaluate the executive director.
   f. Develop personnel policies.
   g. Encourage staff to attend professional meetings, continue to hone their skills
3. Members at large
   a. Understand, support organization's mission.

      b.   Commit time, effort, funds in support of its activities.

      c.   Promote the group and its goals within the community; help recruit members and support.

      d.   Contribute to the group's positive public image.

Roles and Responsibilities of Staff

1. Executive director (COO – chief operating officer)
   a. Facilitate, coordinate, integrate all facets of the organization (its day-to-day operation.)
      · Financial, legal, insurance, tax oversight.
      · Facilities management and maintenance.
      · Community relations, marketing, communication.
      · Personnel development – volunteer and staff.
      · Meeting, program planning and development.
   b. Provide knowledge, skills, expertise, continuity.
   c. Engage in strategic planning with the Board.
   d. Implement policies established by the Board
   e. Consult with, report to the Board regularly.
      · Financial, budgetary, management matters.
      · New technology affecting information, communication, networking.
      · Community issues, government information that may affect the organization.
   f. Represent the organization as interpreter, advocate.
   g. Hire, supervise competent support staff.
   h. Join, participate in appropriate, relevant professional and community associations.

2. Support staff
   • Understand the group's mission, goals with personal support, loyalty.
   • Responsible to the executive director for job description and assignment.
   • Relate assigned tasks to the overall mission.

Principles of Effective Team Building

1. Agreement on goals, mission of the organization.
2. Open and honest communication, climate of trust.
3. Understanding of roles, interdependence, shared leadership.
4. Commitment to group process.

STRATEGIC PLANNING

Strategic Planning is the team-based process by which an organization reaches decisions for future direction.

Purposes
1.   Reaffirms members' understanding of and commitment to the group.
2.   Sets the organization on its future course.
3.   Maximizes resources: personnel, funds, facilities.
4.   Identifies areas to be discussed, developed, changed, improved, eliminated, evaluated.
5.   Strives for effectiveness, efficiency, excellence.
6.   Provides structure for teamwork: leadership, membership, staff.
7.   Establishes priorities for future action.
8.   Improves group's visibility, image: internally (in the organization) and externally (in the community.)
9.   Assesses performance, measures progress.
10. Encourages creativity, leadership skills.

Methods
1.   Establish a strategic planning committee.
2.   Formulate an agreed upon mission statement: a clear statement of the shared vision of the group's purposes and functions (see p. 18).
3.   Assess the organization's current strengths, weaknesses, opportunities, and threats (SWOT analysis).
4.   Determine desired goals and priorities for future directions in various areas:
     • Governance and structure: bylaws, policies, practices.
     • Membership profile; outreach, recruitment, retention, involvement.
     • Programming: programs, activities, projects, services.
     • Communication: publications, announcements, invitations – internal and external; public relations, marketing, use of modern technology.

- Visibility and image: perception of its members and in the community; name recognition
- Finances: dues, fund raising, budgeting (income and expenses).

5. Prioritize suggested goals in each area.
    - Determine strategies for each.
    - Set timetables for action – immediately, one to three years.
    - Decide who will perform the tasks
    - List resources needed: personnel, funds, materials.
    - Monitor the plan(s); review periodically, alter as needed.
6. Implement the agreed upon plan(s).

Evaluation

1. Gather feedback from members and participants.
2. Check to see if goals were accomplished.
3. Assess the process by which the tasks were undertaken and/or completed.
4. Discuss concerns for future endeavors.
5. Report results to the governing body of the organization for future actions.

Benefits of strategic planning

1. Establishes priorities among agreed upon areas of concern.
2. Clarifies desires, needs for future direction.
3. Develops basis for decision making.
4. Allows current decisions based on desired future results.
5. Improves teamwork and expertise among leadership and membership.
6. Builds a common sense of purpose.
7. Allows for problem solving; improves performance.
8. Responds to changing circumstances.
9. Highlights planning processes for short and long term goals.
10. Provides for modification and reassessment periodically.
11. Encourages creativity.

DELEGATING EFFECTIVELY

Delegation provides for leadership training and experience, for sharing responsibilities and should involve members in meaningful tasks.

1. Define objectives, job descriptions.
2. Select people with the necessary skills, knowledge, commitment, enthusiasm.
3. Mutually decide accepted goals, expectations.
4. Maintain open communication with all those involved.
5. Provide background information, relevant material.
6. Be willing to accept new ideas and methods, to trust others' judgement, to take risks.
7. Encourage people to stretch, grow, develop skills.
8. Take mistakes in stride, as learning experiences; evaluate and move forward.
9. Monitor progress without interference or "micromanaging."
10. Be available for consultation, information, support.
11. Praise, compliment success, accomplishment, growth.

APPENDIX

I.   Sample Bylaws

II.   Sample Agenda

III.   Sample Minutes

IV.   Sample Correspondence

V.   Sample Balanced Budget

VI.   Sample News Releases

VII.   Sample Resolutions

VIII.   Sample Evaluation Sheet

APPENDIX I - SAMPLE BYLAWS

Suggestions for filling in the blanks appear in parentheses.

BYLAWS OF THE _____ (Name of organization)

Article I.   NAME
> The name of this organization shall be (The City Library Club) to be referred to in these bylaws as (The Club).

Article II.   OBJECT
> The (object(s), purpose(s)) of this organization shall be:

Section 1.   _____

Section 2.   _____

Article III.   MEMBERS

Section 1.   Any person who _____ shall be eligible to membership_____
(upon payment of dues, or upon having completed application, etc.)

Section 2.   Classes of memberships shall be: _____
(active, associate, non-resident, honorary, etc.; each class should be defined here or in Policy).

Section 3.   The annual dues shall be established by the board from time to time payable in _____ (month). The fiscal year shall be from _____ to _____ (day and month). (Provisions for notification and/or action in cases of delinquency in dues payment may be included in this section or in Policy.)

Section 4.   Any member desiring to resign shall do so _____ (in writing to the secretary, or some other provision).

Article IV.   OFFICERS

Section 1.   The officers of (The Club) shall be _____ (list the officers).

Section 2.   Candidates for office shall be nominated by _____. (State whom and when,

---

The nomoinating committee may be described in a separate section in ARTICLE VIII. Committees.

such as: the membership at its March meeting <u>or</u> by a nominating committee appointed/or elected to prepare a slate of officers and board members to be presented for election at the Annual Meeting.) The nominating committee shall consist of _____ members, (number and classes of members as: two members of the board and three members at large, always an odd number). The report of the nominating committee shall be _____ (presented/published) no later than _____ (days) before the Annual Meeting. Additional nominations may be made _____ (in writing to…or from the floor no later than <u>10 days</u> before the Annual Meeting.)

Section 3. Officers shall be elected at the Annual Meeting in _____ (month) for a term of _____ or until their successors are elected (or installed) and assume office. (If all officers are not elected the same year, or if election is to be by ballot, provisions are made in this section.)

Section 4. (This section states eligibility for office, succession in office and/or restrictions such as "No officer shall be eligible to serve for more than two consecutive terms in the same office" or, "Any qualified member may be eligible for office". May also add here or in Policy "A member serving an unexpired term shall be eligible for election for a full term.")

Section 5. Duties of officers (may become a separate article).

    a. The president shall preside at all meetings of (The Club) and the board of directors; be a member ex-officio of all committees except the nominating committee; appoint all committee chairmen (except those who may be elected); be a co-signer of all checks and bank accounts (and any other specific duties).

    b. The (first) vice president* shall perform the duties of the president in the absence of that officer. (In addition, list any other specific duties. If more than one vice president, list any prescribed duties of each.)

    c. The recording secretary shall keep the minutes

---

*The term executive vice president is used to refer to a paid director.

of all meetings of (The Club) and the board of directors. (List any other duties here, such as keeping record of attendance.)

d. The corresponding secretary shall conduct the general correspondence of (The Club); send notices of all board and general meetings;…

e. The treasurer shall be custodian of all funds of (The Club); keep an itemized account of all receipts and disbursements; disburse funds in payment of authorized expenditures, (state how authorized), be a co-signer with _____ (the president) of all checks. (list any other specific duties such as notifying members delinquent in dues payments; bonding arrangements and provisions for an annual audit may be included.)

f. (Any other officers should be listed, such as financial secretary, auditor, etc.)

Section 6. Vacancies in office shall be filled by _____ (a standing nominating committee or the board of directors).

Article V. BOARD OF DIRECTORS

Section 1. The board of directors shall consist of _____ . (List members, as: the elected officers, the immediate or all past presidents and (number) elected and up to (number) appointed board members. (Include how elected or appointed and length of term. Usually with a two-year term, one-half the prescribed number will be elected each year.)

Section 2. The board of directors shall supervise the affairs of (The Club) between general meetings. (Add any other powers or duties to be invested in the board, such as: may make recommendations to the membership for action.)

Section 3. The board of directors shall meet at least _____ times a year. Special meetings of the board may be called by _____ (the president) and shall be called upon the request of _____ members of the board.

Section 4. _____ (number) members shall constitute a quorum for board meetings. (A majority is required unless a lesser number is stated here.)

Article VI.   EXECUTIVE COMMITTEE (if there is to be one)
Section 1.   The executive committee shall consist of _____.
              (List the members such as: the elected officers and
              the immediate past president; may include the execu-
              tive director, if applicable.)
Section 2.   The executive committee shall supervise the affairs of
              (The Club) between board meetings, act in emer-
              gency situations and make recommendations to the
              board for action. Reports of executive committee
              action shall be made to the board.
Section 3.   Meetings of the executive committee may be called
              by the president and shall be called upon the written
              request of _____ (number) members.
Section 4.   _____ (number) members of the executive
              committee shall constitute a quorum. (The number
              chosen is usually half.)

Article VII.   MEETINGS (regular, special, Annual Meeting, quorum)
Section 1.   There shall be at least _____ (number) of general
              meetings of (The Club) each year to be held
              _____(when). In case of emergency, an alter-
              nate date may be set by _____ (the board of
              directors or executive committee or the president in
              consultation with the other officers, or
              _____).
Section 2.   The Annual Meeting shall take place in _____
              (month) for the purpose of the election (and installa-
              tion) of officers and for receiving all annual reports.
Section 3.   Special meetings of _____ (The Club) may
              be called by _____ (the board of directors, the
              executive committee, the president) and shall be
              called upon the written request of _____ members
              (about the same number as the quorum).
Section 4.   _____ members shall constitute a quorum for all
              meetings of (The Club). (The quorum should be
              realistic, usually about one-fifth of the active
              membership.)

Article VIII. COMMITTEES
Section 1.   The standing committees shall be _____ (list
              alphabetically as: membership, program, ways and
              means, etc. Add a provision for the establishment of

other committees which may be named by the board of directors as the need arises.)

Section 2.   Special or "ad hoc" committees may be established as needs arise and are disbanded when their work is completed.

Section 3.   Committee chairmen shall be _____ (usually appointed by the president) to serve for a period of one year or until the next Annual Meeting. (Duties of committees are not enumerated in bylaws, but may be established by written policy, or rules of procedure.)

Section 4.   (Departmentalization may be provided for here, listing the departments alphabetically as: The work of _____ (The Club) shall be divided into departments _____ (Administrative, Fund Raising, Programming, etc.), each under the coordination/supervision of a vice-president.)

Article IX   FISCAL MANAGEMENT

Officers and directors' indemnification.
Responsibility for assets and liabilities, management of real estate (if applicable) can be included here.

Article X.   PARLIAMENTARY AUTHORITY

Robert's Rules of Order, Newly Revised shall govern (The Club) on all matters not covered by these bylaws and/or any other special rules which may be adopted.

Article XI.   AMENDMENT PROCEDURE

These bylaws may be amended at _____ (any regular, although usually at the Annual Meeting) of the organization by a 2/3 vote of the members present and voting, provided that notice of the proposed amendment(s) has been given in writing, not less than _____ days before the meeting at which such amendment(s) will be presented for action.

APPENDIX II – SAMPLE AGENDA

The agenda is the order of business, the schedule, of a meeting or assembly. The agenda for the next meeting may be mailed to participants with the minutes of the previous meeting; in addition, reports to be considered may be included in the mailing for knowledge and consideration in preparation for the meeting.

1. Call to order by the presiding officer.
2. National anthem if customary; other anthems precede the Star Spangled Banner.
3. Welcome; prayer (optional).
4. Quorum check; the quorum is the number of members necessary to be present in order to transact business (should be stated in Bylaws).
5. Minutes of preceding meeting of the same body:
   a. May have been mailed; call for additions, corrections, approval.
   b. May be read by recording secretary to be corrected and approved, dated and signed by recording secretary.
   c. Reading may be dispensed with upon motion, but must be approved, dated and signed by at least three members who had been present at the recorded meeting.
6. Correspondence: action may be taken on items as presented.
7. Treasurer's report: presented, open to queries, copy attached to minutes and filed for audit.
8. President's report: includes meetings attended as representative of the group, announcements of general interest and:
   a. Report(s) of executive committee meetings, if any, to the board.
   b. Report(s) of board action to the membership.
   c. Recommendations for action (from a. or b. above), usually presented by the recording secretary.
9. Executive director's report, if applicable and customary.
10. Other officers' reports.
11. Timely committee reports: standing and special; name of committee and presenter.
12. Unfinished business: action deferred from previous meeting(s); president may bring item(s) forward, or any member may ask for an update.

13. New business.
14. Good and welfare, if customary.
15. Program, if any; presiding officer introduces chairman who introduces the program.
16. Adjournment by presiding officer.

PRACTICAL AGENDA AIDS

1. Mail agenda to members in advance.
2. Enclose background information on key items to be proposed for action.
3. Notify those who are expected to report; ascertain if discussion/action will be called for to allow time.
4. Plan timing for key items to be proposed when the largest attendance is expected.

APPENDIX III - SAMPLE MINUTES

Minutes of the City Library Club, Inc. – January 5, 0000

The regular meeting of the City Library Club, Inc. was called to order by the president, James Cochran, on Tuesday, January 5, 0000, at 7:30 p.m. in the River Room of the Uptown Library.

Those present were: (list names)

The minutes of the December meeting were approved as distributed.

Correspondence: presented by Audrey Marshall, corresponding secretary.
1.   Letter of resignation from Janet Jacklin; accepted with regret.
2.   Letter of thanks from the Tiny Tots Nursery for books presented in November.
3.   Announcement of State Library Association Convention at the Civic Center on March 9, and letter asking for names of delegates. Thelma King moved that the president and vice president attend as official delegates and that their registration fees be paid from the contingency fund; motion seconded and passed. The suggestion was made that the club budget each year for the registration fee of at least one delegate to the State Association's Annual Convention. The matter was referred to the Board.

Treasurer's report by Freda Johnson, treasurer:

Balance in Union Bank, December 1, 0000		$675.82
Receipts for December		
Dues	$50.00	
Contributions	$35.00	
		$ 85.00
		$760.82
Disbursements		
Printing and postage	$ 25.00	
Refreshments	$ 20.15	
Holiday story sessions	$150.00	
		($195.15)
Current Balance (January 5, 0000)		$565.67

Report was filed for audit.

President's report:

The president attended the fall board meeting of the State Library Association at which time he was made acutely aware of the continuing need to support school libraries and to educate the public as to these needs, especially in schools with no active P.T.A.'s and/or no regular allocations for library services. He urged as many members as possible to attend the evening meeting of the State Convention to be held March 9, at which time Dr. William Anderson of the National Library Association will report on the survey made last year entitled "The State of our State Libraries."

Board recommendation:

Marian McGee, secretary, read the following recommendation passed by the Board at its December meeting: that the Club authorize the expenditure of an additional $50.00 ($150.00 having been earmarked in the budget) for the purchase of children's books for the recently dedicated lending library at the Central Avenue Community Center. She moved the adoption of the recommendation. After discussion, the motion was passed.

Committee reports:

Membership – in the absence of chairman Barbara Bland, Carol Flowers reported ten new members, one resignation, making a total membership of 146.

Holiday Story hours – Morton Morris, chairman, thanked all who worked on this project and reported excellent attendance at all five sessions. The committee will hold an evaluation meeting later this month and make its final report at the February meeting.

New business:

Maynard Jones announced that he has been contacted by the principal of School No. 30 on Beech St., which seems to be in desperate need of books since the wave of vandalism last summer. After much discussion it was agreed that Mr. Jones arrange a meeting with the principal, the Club president and extension chairman to ascertain the school's needs and eligibility for books under Club policy. A report of this meeting will be presented in February.

Program:

    Mary Patterson, program chairman, introduced Dr. Clara Campbell who spoke on "Classic Comics: Cure or Curse?" Her presentation was followed by a question and answer period. The announcement was made that next month's program – a "Meet-The-Author" night will be held on Tuesday, February 7.

The meeting was adjourned at 9:45 p.m.

Helen A. Harper
Secretary

Approved February 7, 2000
H.A.H.

APPENDIX IV – SAMPLE CORRESPONDENCE

(Letter of resignation and letter accepting resignation of a Board Member)

Dear Audrey,

It is with regret that I find it necessary to resign from the Board of
_____. I have felt it an honor and a rewarding experience to serve as a
Board member. Now, because _____, it will impossible for me to attend
meetings regularly and fulfill the obligations of a Board member. I will certainly
maintain membership in the Club because of my continued interest in its important
work.

Please convey my regrets to the other officers and members of the Board.
Best wishes for a successful year!

Sincerely,

Janet Jacklin

* * * * * * * * * * *

Dear Janet,

At its regular meeting on Tuesday night, January 5, the Board accepted
your resignation with regret.

We acknowledge with grateful appreciation the time and energy you have
contributed during your term on the Board, especially the outstanding job you did
as chairman of the _____ committee last year. Although we understand
that it is impossible for you to continue as a Board member at this time, we do hope
that in the future you will be able to become active once again.

Sincerely,

Audrey Marshall,
Corresponding Secretary

APPENDIX V – SAMPLE BALANCED BUDGET

Estimated income
    Dues $500.00
    Contributions   150.00
    Fund raising events
        Donor $1,000.00
        Sales   250.00   1,250.00 $1,900.00

Estimated income			
Dues		$500.00	
Contributions		150.00	
Fund raising events			
Donor	$1,000.00		
Sales	250.00	1,250.00	$1,900.00

Estimated expenditures		
Administrative printing and postage	$_____	
Programs	$_____	
Publicity		$_____
Contributions and dues		
_____ $_____		
_____ $_____		
_____ $_____		
	$_____	
Projects		
_____ $_____		
_____ $_____		
_____ $_____		
	$_____	
Attendance at conferences	$_____	
Miscellaneous	$_____	$1,900.00

APPENDIX VI – SAMPLE NEWS RELEASES

I.   **SAMPLE NEWSPAPER RELEASE (by e-mail or mail)**
Organization letterhead

From	FOR RELEASE
Name	SEPTEMBER 20
Title	
Address	
City, State	
Phone #	
Fax #	

School-For-A-Day, an annual event of the Women' Leadership
Council, will be held on Thursday, October 9, 2002, at the
Community College Library. Registration will begin at 9:00 a.m.,
the day's program at 9:30 a.m.
Members of all constituent organizations have been invited to
participate in a series of workshops designed to enhance their
leadership skills and their group's effectiveness.
(Name, Title) will give the keynote address. Morning workshops
will include panel discussions concerning membership and
leadership recruitment. The afternoon sessions from 1:00 p.m. to
4:00 p.m. will include fundraising and publicity techniques.
Registration fee, including lunch, is $ _____.
(Name) is president of the Council. Reservations may be made by
mail to the Council office at (Address) by e-mail (____ @ ____)
or by calling (Name, phone #) or (Name, phone #) by (Deadline
Date).

II. SAMPLE RADIO/TV RELEASE

Organization Letterhead
PUBLIC SERVICE ANNOUNCEMENT

Name   FOR RELEASE

Title   WEEK OF

Address

_____

City, State

Phone #

Fax #

The State Library Association will hold its Annual Convention, Thursday, March 9, 2001, at 8:00 p.m. at the Central Library on Main Street. Dr. William Anderson of the National Library Association will report results of the comprehensive survey completed in 2000, entitled "The State of Our State Libraries." The public is invited to attend.

APPENDIX VII – SAMPLE RESOLUTIONS

I.   **A SIMPLE RESOLUTION:**

RESOLVED, That the City Library Club urges and publicly endorses the establishment of a neighborhood library in the new subdivision of Mayberry, as its major project for the new year, and upon its becoming a reality, pledges to raise funds to help furnish a children's reading room.

II.   **A RESOLUTION WITH A PREAMBLE:**

Whereas, The City Library Club has worked diligently throughout the years toward the development of the excellent branch library system in the city; and

Whereas, The Club has continuing interest in the establishment of branch libraries in every subdivision of the city; and

Whereas, There are at present no plans for a library facility in Mayberry, the new subdivision in the northwest corridor; therefore, be it

RESOLVED, That the City Library Club make the establishment of a library facility in Mayberry its major project for the coming year; and further, be it

RESOLVED, That the City Library Club urges the Mayor and City Council, the Central Library Board and the developers of Mayberry to provide space and start-up funds for a library facility to become a reality within the next calendar year; and further, be it

RESOLVED, That the City Library Club will raise funds to help furnish a children's reading room.

APPENDIX VIII – SAMPLE EVALUATION SHEET

(May be adjusted for workshops, programs, special events, etc.)

Title of event/workshop _____

Leader, presenters _____   _____

_____   _____

Goals, objectives

_____

_____

Were the stated goals met?

_____

_____

Did the workshop/event meet your expectations?

_____

_____

What was most helpful?

_____

_____

What was the least helpful?

_____

_____

How do you rate the workshop leader, presenters? (Knowledge? Content? Overall presentation?) Check one:
_____Excellent_____Good _____Fair_____Poor

Comments:

_____

_____

Suggestions for future workshops/events:

_____

_____

Thank you for your feedback!

NOTES

NOTES

Printed in the United States
44405LVS00002B/1-267

9 780824 127183